Mr. Punch At The S[illegible]

Charles Keene

PUNCH LIBRARY OF HUMOUR

Edited by J. A. HAMMERTON

Designed to provide in a series of volumes, each complete in itself, the cream of national humour, contributed by the masters of comic draughtsmanship and the leading wits of the age to "Punch," from its beginning in 1841 to the present day

MR. PUNCH AT THE SEASIDE

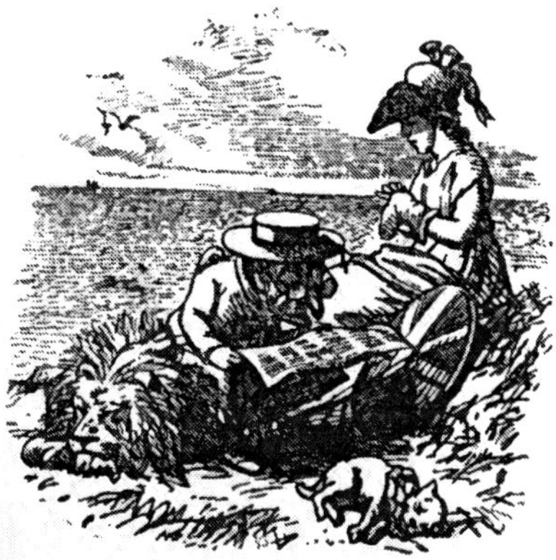

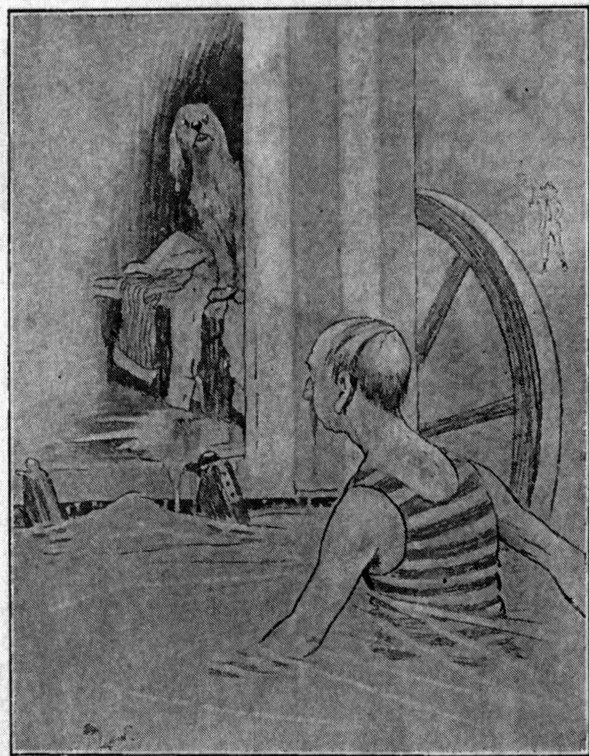

"BY THE SILVER SEA"

This is *not* Jones's dog.

MR. PUNCH AT THE SEASIDE

AS PICTURED BY

CHARLES KEENE, JOHN LEECH, GEORGE DU MAURIER, PHIL MAY, L. RAVEN-HILL, J. BERNARD PARTRIDGE, GORDON BROWNE, E. T. REED, AND OTHERS . .

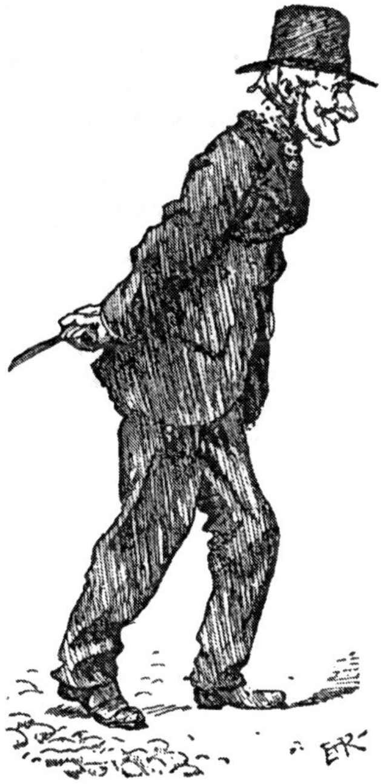

WITH 200 ILLUSTRATIONS

PUBLISHED BY ARRANGEMENT WITH

THE PROPRIETORS OF "PUNCH"

THE EDUCATIONAL BOOK CO. LTD.

THE PUNCH LIBRARY OF HUMOUR

Twenty-five volumes, crown 8vo, 192 pages fully illustrated

LIFE IN LONDON
COUNTRY LIFE
IN THE HIGHLANDS
SCOTTISH HUMOUR
IRISH HUMOUR
COCKNEY HUMOUR
IN SOCIETY
AFTER DINNER STORIES
IN BOHEMIA
AT THE PLAY
MR. PUNCH AT HOME
ON THE CONTINONG
RAILWAY BOOK
AT THE SEASIDE
MR. PUNCH AFLOAT
IN THE HUNTING FIELD
MR. PUNCH ON TOUR
WITH ROD AND GUN
MR. PUNCH AWHEEL
BOOK OF SPORTS
GOLF STORIES
IN WIG AND GOWN
ON THE WARPATH
BOOK OF LOVE
WITH THE CHILDREN

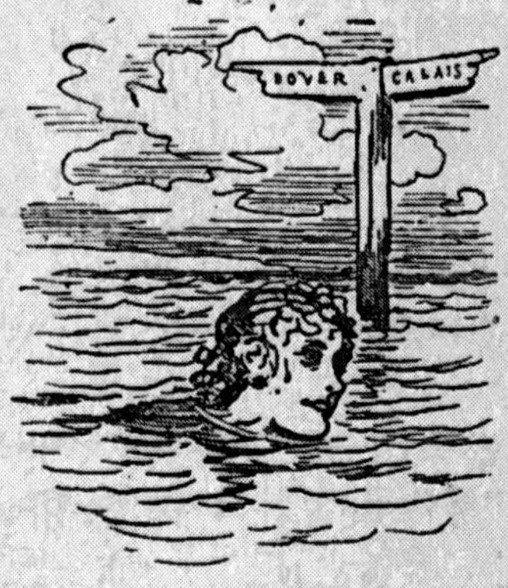

EDITOR'S NOTE

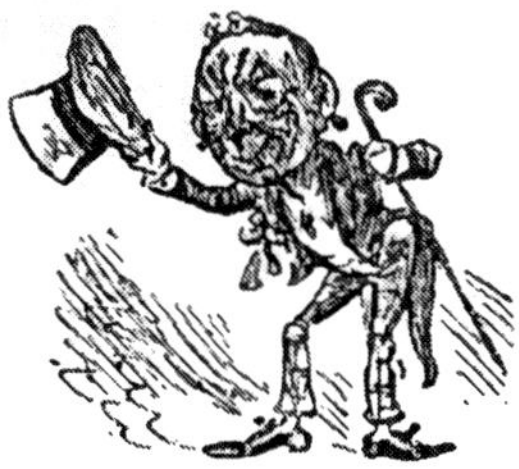

ONE of the leading characteristics of the nineteenth century was the tremendous change effected in the social life of Great Britain by the development of cheap railway travel. The annual holiday at the seaside speedily became as inevitable a part of the year's progress as the milkman's morning call is of the day's routine. What at first had been a rare and memorable event in a lifetime developed into a habit, to which, with our British love for conventions, all of us conform.

Whether or not our French critics are justified in saying that we Britishers take our pleasures sadly, these pages from the seaside chronicles of Mr. Punch will bear witness, and while at times they may seem to support the case of our critics, at others the evidence is eloquent against them. This at least is certain, that whatever the temperament of the British as displayed during the holiday season at our popular resorts, the point of view of our national jester, Mr. Punch, is unfailingly humorous, and such sadness as some of our countrymen may bring to their pleasures is but food for the mirth of merry Mr. Punch, who, we are persuaded, stands for the sum total of John Bull's good humour in his outlook on the life of his countrymen.

As the real abstract and brief chronicler of our time, Mr. Punch has mirrored in little the social history of the last sixty-five years, and apart from the genuine entertainment which this book presents, it is scarcely less instructive as a pictorial history of British manners during this period. One may here follow in the vivid sketches of the master-draughtsmen of the age the ceaseless and bewildering changes of fashion — the passing of the crinoline, the coming and going of the bustle, the chignon, and similar vanities, and the evolution of the present-day styles of dress both of men and women.

It is also curious to notice how little seaside customs, amusements, troubles and delights, have varied in the last half-century. Landladies are at the end what they were at the beginning; the same old type of bathing-machine is still in use; our forefathers and their womenfolk in the days when Mr. Punch was young behaved themselves by "the silver sea" just as their children's children do to-day. Nothing has changed, except that the most select of seaside places is no longer so select as it was in the pre-railway days, and that the wealthier classes, preferring the attractions of Continental resorts, are less in evidence at our own watering-places.

The motto of this little work, as of all those in the series to which it belongs, is "Our true intent is all for your delight," but if the book carry with it some measure of instruction, we trust that may not be the less to its credit.

MR. PUNCH AT THE SEASIDE

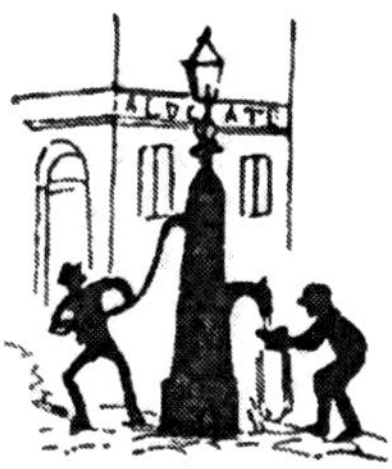

A FASHIONABLE WATERING PLACE

Mrs. Dorset (*of "Dorset's Sugar and Butter Stores," Mile End Road*). "Why on earth can't we go to a more *dressy* place than this, 'Enery? I'm sick of this dreary 'ole, year after year. It's nothing but sand and water, sand and water!"

Mr. Dorset. "If it wasn't for sand and water, you wouldn't get no 'olerday."

SEASIDE MEM.—The Society recently started to abolish Tied-houses will not include Bathing Machines within the scope of its operations.

"WHERE'S RAMSGATE?"

[*Mr. Justice Hawkins.* Where is Ramsgate?
Mr. Dickens. It is in Thanet, your lordship.
Report of Twyman v. *Bligh.*]

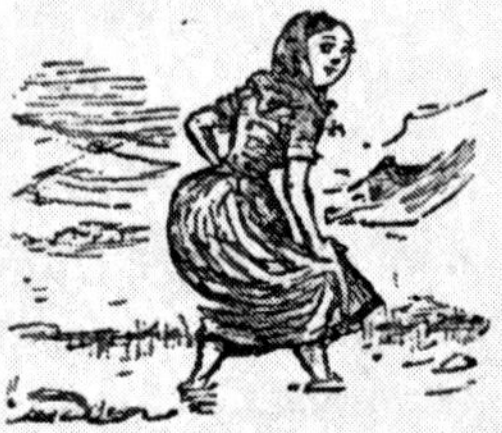

BIDDY-FORD

"WHERE'S Ramsgate?" Justice Hawkins cried.
"Where on our earthly planet?"
The learned Dickens straight replied,
"'Tis in the Isle of Thanet.

"Ramsgate is where the purest air
Will make your head or leg well
Will jaded appetite repair,
With the shrimp cure of Pegwell.

"Where's Ramsgate? It is near the place
Where Julius Cæsar waded,
And nearer still to where his Grace
Augustine come one day did.

"All barristers should Ramsgate know:
I speak of it with pleasure,"
Quoth Dickens. "There I often go
When wanting a refresher.

"Where's Ramsgate? Where I've often seen
Both S-mb-rne and Du M-r-*er*,
When I have gone by 3.15
Granville Express, Victori*er*.

"With Thanet Harriers, when you are
   Well mounted on a pony,
You'll say, for health who'd go so far
   As Cannes, Nice, or Mentone?

"With Poland, of the Treasury,
   Recorder eke of Dover,
I oft go down for pleasurey.
   Alack! 'tis too soon over!

"O'er Thanet's Isle where'er you trudge,
   My Lud, you'll find no land which——"
"Dickens take Ramsgate!" quote the Judge.
   "Luncheon! I'm off to Sandwich!"

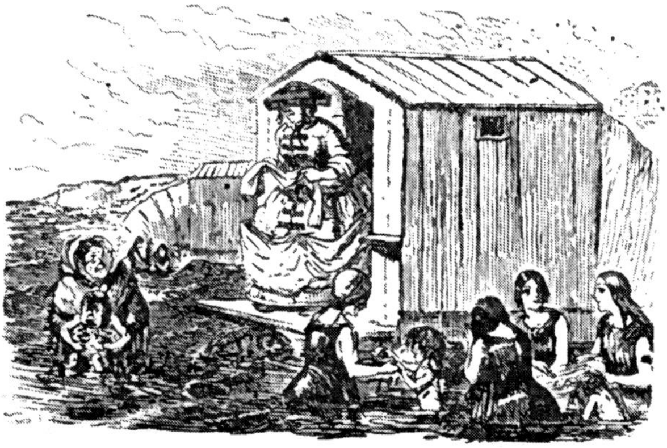

A JUDGE BY APPEARANCE

Bathing Guide. "Bless 'is 'art! I know'd he'd take to it kindly—by the werry looks on 'im!"

THE WONDERS OF THE SEA-SHORE

Contributed by "GLAUCUS," *who is staying at a quiet watering-place, five miles from anywhere, and three miles from a Railway Station.*

Monday (?) after breakfast, lying on the beach.

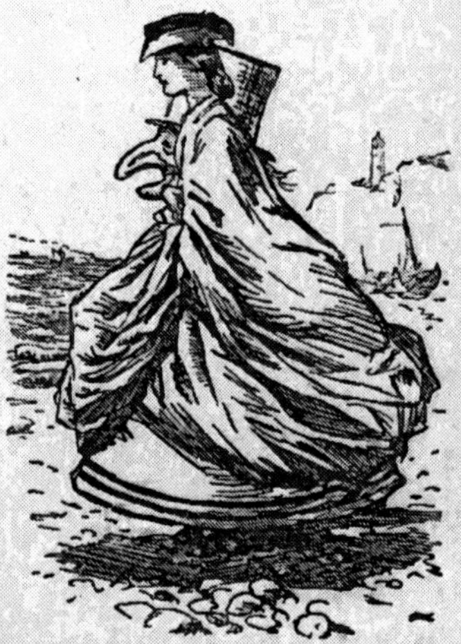

WONDER if it is Monday, or Tuesday?

Wonder what time it is?

Wonder if it will be a fine day?

Wonder what I shall do if it is? On second thoughts, wonder what I shall do if it isn't?

Wonder if there are any letters?

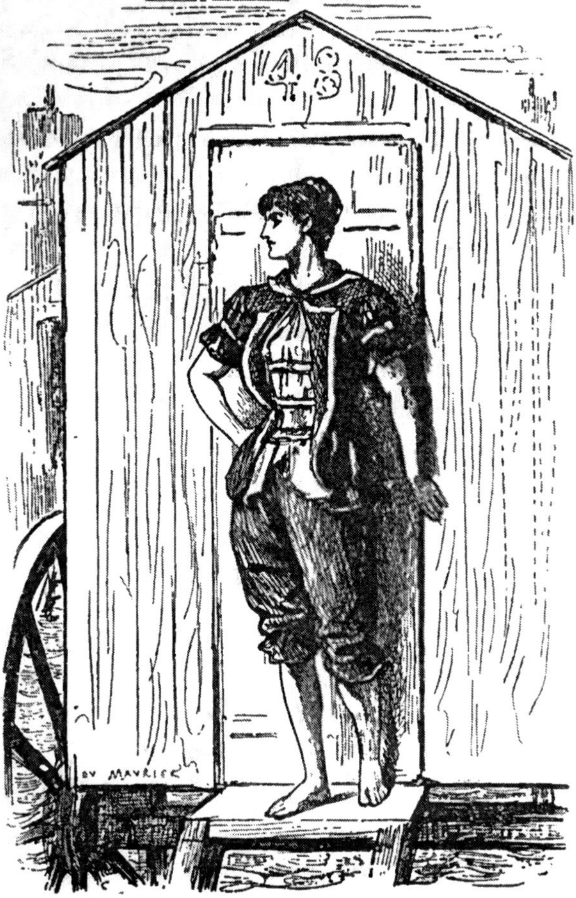

DEA EX MACHINÂ!
(*A Reminiscence*)

Wonder who that is in a white petticoat with her hair down?

Wonder if she came yesterday or the day before?

Wonder if she's pretty?

Wonder what I've been thinking about the last ten minutes?

Wonder how the boatmen here make a livelihood by lying all day at full length on the beach?

Wonder why every one who sits on the shore throws pebbles into the sea?

Wonder what there is for dinner?

Wonder what I shall do all the afternoon?

Same day, after lunch, lying on the beach.

Wonder who in the house beside myself is partial to my dry sherry?

Wonder what there is for dinner?

Wonder what's in the paper to-day?

Wonder if it's hot in London? Should say it was.

Wonder how I ever could live in London?

Wonder if there's any news from America?

Wonder what tooral looral means in a chorus?

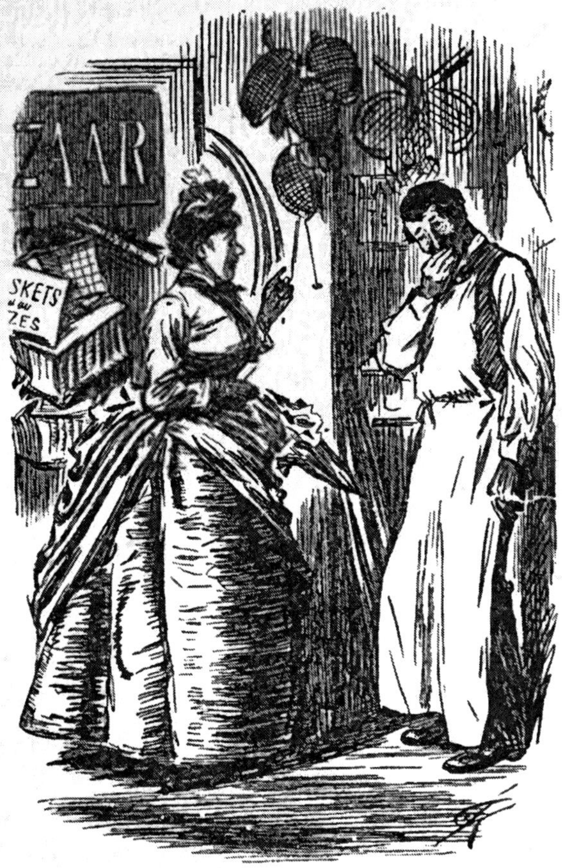

SHOPPING

Lady (*at Seaside* "*Emporium*"). "How much are those —ah—improvers?"

Shopman. "Improv—hem! — They're not, ma'am"— (*confused*)—"not — not the article you require, ma'am. They're fencing-masks, ma'am!" [*Tableau!*

Children playing near me, pretty, very?

Wonder if that little boy intended to hit me on the nose with a stone?

Wonder if he's going to do it again? Hope not.

Wonder if I should like to be a shrimp?

Same day, after an early dinner, lying on the beach

Wonder why I can never get any fish?

Wonder why my landlady introduces cinders into the gravy?

Wonder more than ever who there is at my lodgings so partial to my dry sherry?

Wonder if that's the coast of France in the distance?

Feel inclined for a quiet conversation with my fellow-man.

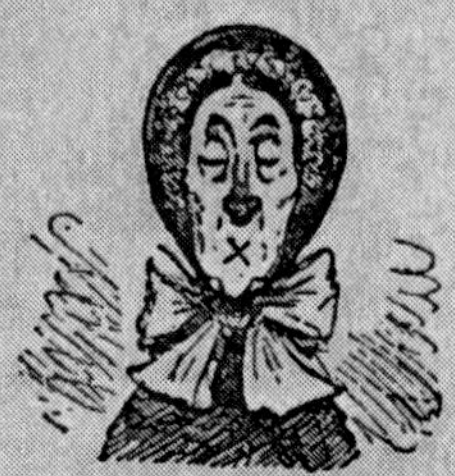

EXMOUTH

A boatman approaches. I wonder (to the boatman) if it will be a fine day to-morrow? He wonders too? We both wonder together?

Wonder (again to the boat-man) if the rail will make

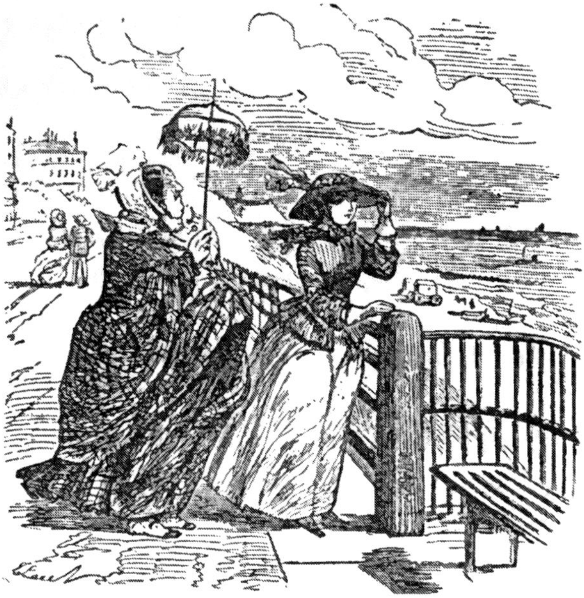

A LARGE BUMP OF CAUTION

Flora. "Oh, let us sit here, aunt, the breeze is so delightful."

Aunt. "Yes—it's very nice, I dare say; but I won't come any nearer to the cliff, for I am always afraid of *slipping through those railings!*"

much difference to the place? He shakes his head and says "Ah! he wonders!" and leaves me.

Wonder what age I was last birthday?

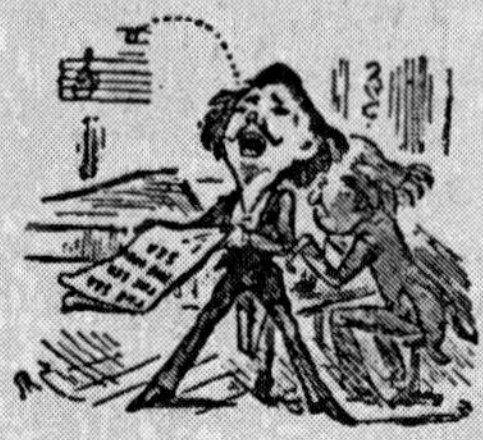

A HIGH SEA OVER THE BAR

Wonder if police inspectors are as a rule fond of bathing?

Wonder what gave me that idea?

Wonder what I shall do all this evening?

Same day, after supper, Moonlight, lying on the beach.

Wonder if there ever was such a creature as a mermaid?

Wonder several times more than ever who it is that's so fond of my dry sherry?

Wonder if the Pope can swim?

Wonder what made me think of that?

Wonder if I should like to go up in a balloon?

Wonder what Speke and Grant had for dinner to-day?

Wonder if the Zoological Gardens are open at sunrise?

Wonder what I shall do to-morrow?

FRUIT TO BE AVOIDED BY BATHERS.—Currants.

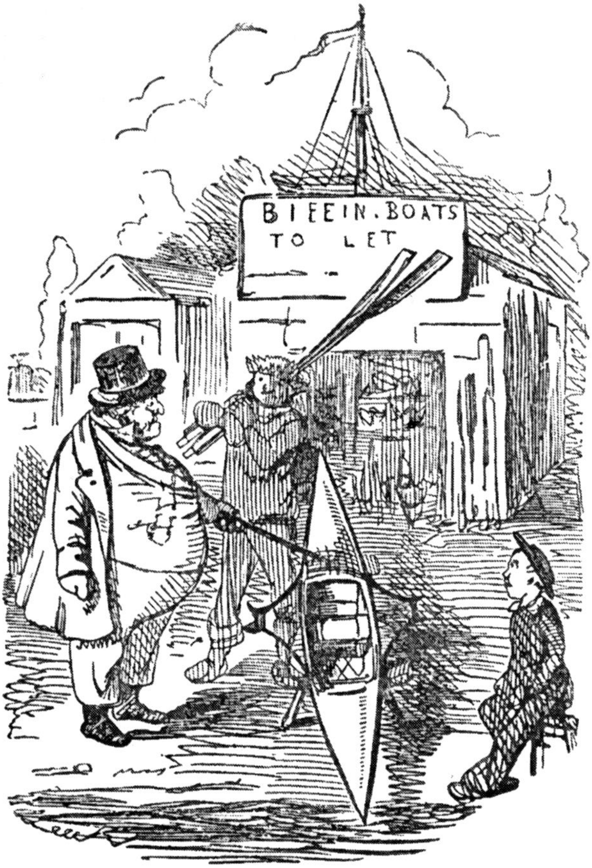

A BOAT FOR AN HOUR

Stout Gentleman. "What! is that the only boat you have in?"

A SEASIDE REVERIE

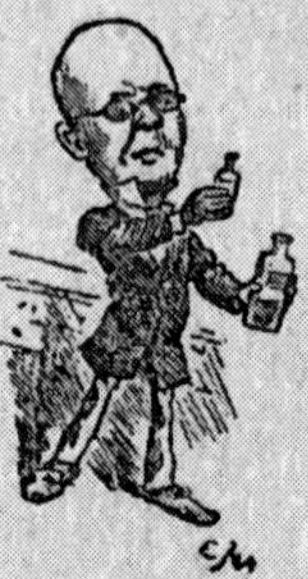

I THINK, as I sit at my ease on the
 shingle,
 And list to the musical voice of the
 Sea,
How gaily my Landlady always will
 mingle
 From my little caddy her matutine
 tea.
And vainly the bitter remembrance I
 banish
 Of mutton just eaten, my heart is full sore,
To think after one cut it's certain to vanish,
 And never be seen on my board any more.

Some small store of spirit to moisten my throttle
 I keep, and indulge in it once in a way;
But, bless you, it seems to fly out of the bottle
 And swiftly decrease, though untouched all the day.
My sugar and sardines, my bread and my butter,
 Are eaten, and vainly I fret and I frown;
My Landlady, just like an Æsthete's too utter
 A fraud, and I vow that I'll go back to Town.

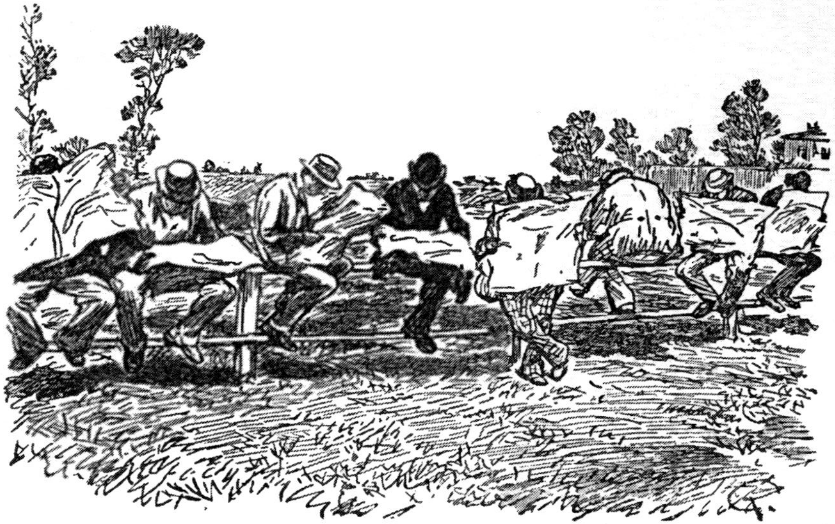

THE MORNING PAPERS

Sketch from our window, 10 a.m., at Sludgeborough Ness.

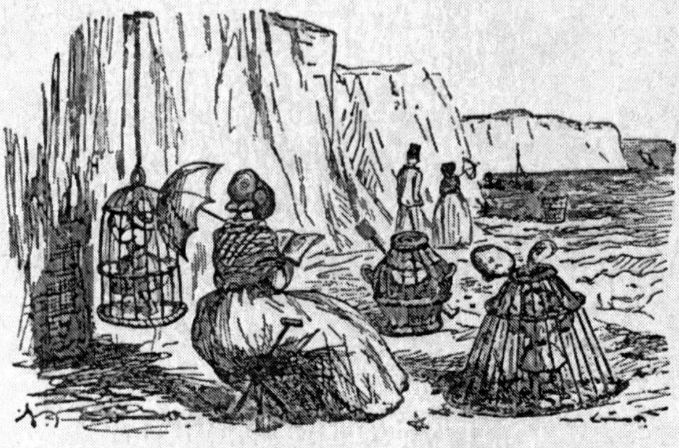

THE NURSEMAID'S FRIEND

SCIENCE has given us the baby-jumper, by which we are enabled to carry out the common exclamation of "Hang those noisy children" without an act of infanticide, by suspending our youngsters in the air; and perhaps allowing them to have their full swing, without getting into mischief; but the apparatus for the nursery will not be complete until we have something in the shape of coops for our pretty little chickens, when they are "out with nurse," and she happens to have something better —or worse—to do than to look after them.

How often, in a most interesting part of a novel, or in the midst of a love passage of real life,

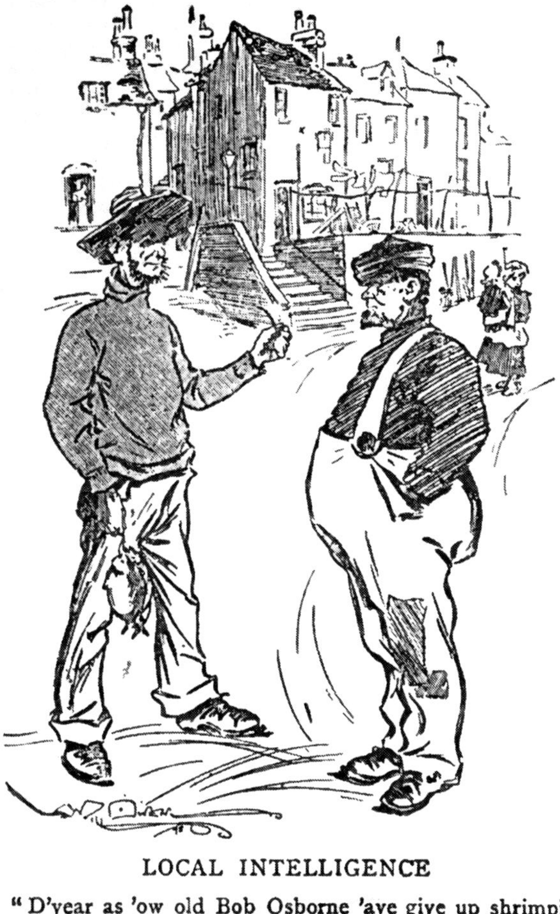

LOCAL INTELLIGENCE

"D'year as 'ow old Bob Osborne 'ave give up shrimpin' an took ter winklin'?"

"Well, I'm blest!"

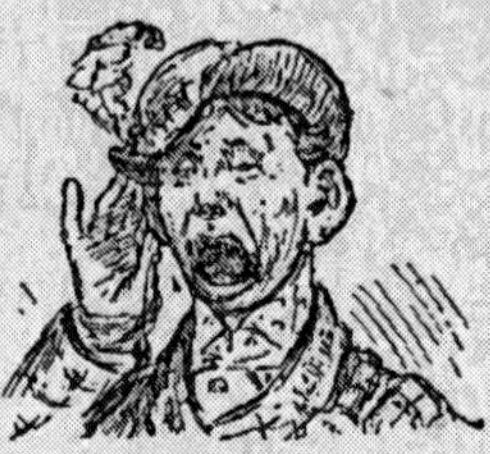

YARMOUTH

in which the nurse is herself the heroine, how often, alas! is she not liable to be disturbed by the howl of a brat, with a cow's horn in his eye, a dog's teeth in his heels, or in some other awkward dilemma, which could not have arisen had the domestic Child-coop been an article of common use in the Metropolitan parks, or on the sands at the seaside?

There is something very beautiful in the comparison of helpless infancy to a brood of young chickens, with its attendant imagery of "mother's wing," and all that sort of thing, but the allegory would be rendered much more complete by the application of the hencoop to domestic purposes. We intend buying one for our own stud of *piccoli*—which means little pickles—and we hope to see all heads of families taking it into their heads to follow our example.

MIDSUMMER MADNESS.—Going to the seaside in search of quiet.

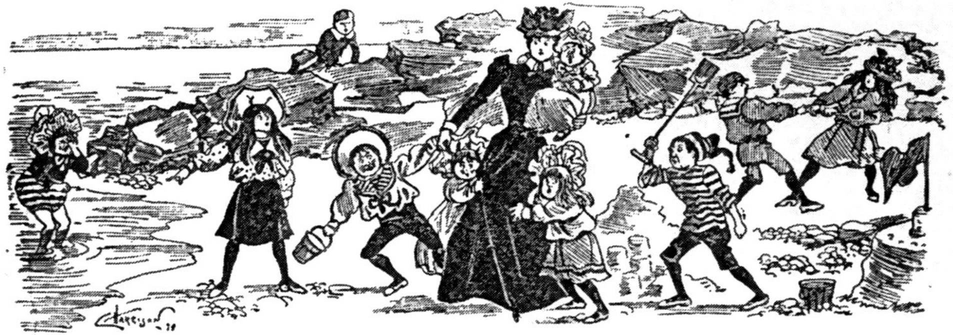

THE INGRATITUDE OF SOME SERVANTS

You give them a change by taking them to the seaside—all they have to do is to look after the children—and yet they don't seem to appreciate it.

ON THE SPOT

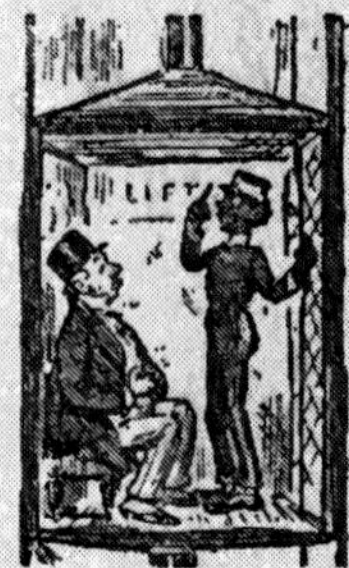

A NATIVE HOISTER

SHALL we like Pierpoint, to which favourite and healthy sea-side resort we finally resolved to come, after a period of much indecision and uncertainty, and where we arrived, in heavy rain, in two cabs, with thirteen packages, on Saturday?

Shall we be comfortable at 62, Convolution Street, dining-room floor, two guineas and a half a week, and all and perhaps rather more than the usual extras?

Shall we like Mrs. Kittlespark?

Shall we find Kate all that a Kate ought to be?

Shall we lock everything up, or repose a noble confidence in Mrs. Kittlespark and Kate?

Shall we get to know the people in the drawing-room?

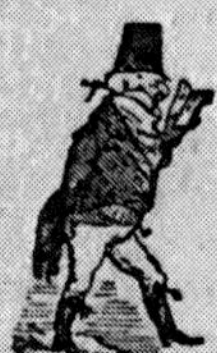

GOING DOWN TO A WATERING PLACE

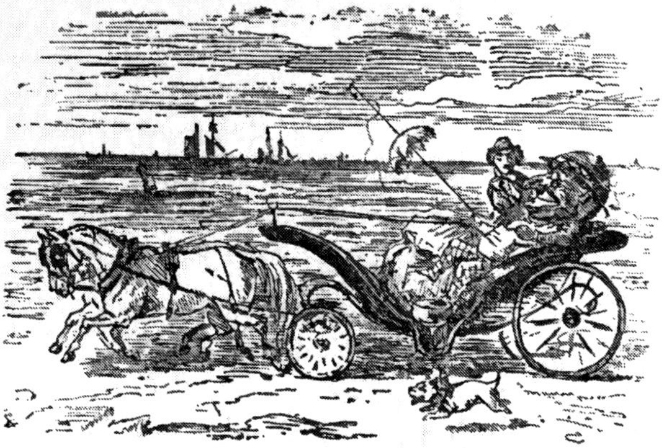

WHAT WE COULD BEAR A GOOD DEAL OF

Shall we subscribe to the Pier, or pay each time we go on it?

Shall we subscribe to that most accommodating Circulating Library, Pigram's, where we can exchange our books at pleasure, *but not oftener than once a day?*

Shall we relax our minds with the newest novels, or give our intellects a bracing course of the best standard works?

Shall we dine late or early?

Shall we call on the Denbigh Flints, who, according to the *Pierpoint Pioneer*, are staying at 10, Ocean Crescent?

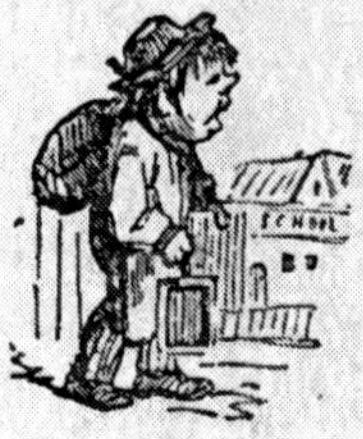
GOING TO BRIGHTON

Shall we carefully avoid the Wilkiesons, whom the same unerring guide reports at 33, Blue Lion Street?

Shall we be satisfied with our first weekly bill?

Shall we find in it any unexpected and novel extras, such as knife-cleaning, proportion of the water-rate, loan of latch-key, &c.?

Shall we get our meat at Round's, who displays the Prince of Wales's Feathers over his shop door, and plumes himself on being "purveyor" to His Royal Highness; or at Cleaver's, who boasts of the patronage of the Hereditary Grand Duke of Seltersland?

Shall we find everything dearer here than it is at home?

Shall we be happy in our laundress?

Shall we be photographed?

Shall we, as Mrs. Kittlespark has a spare bed-room, invite our Cousin Amelia Staythorp,

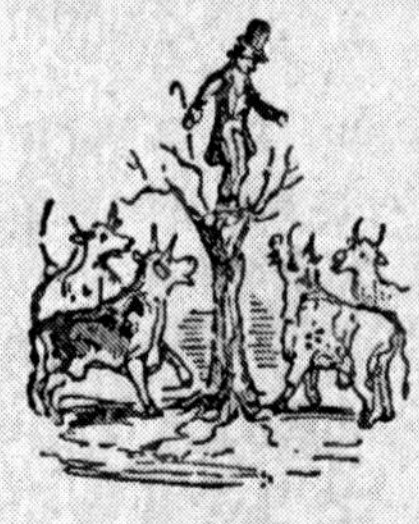
A VIEW OF COWES

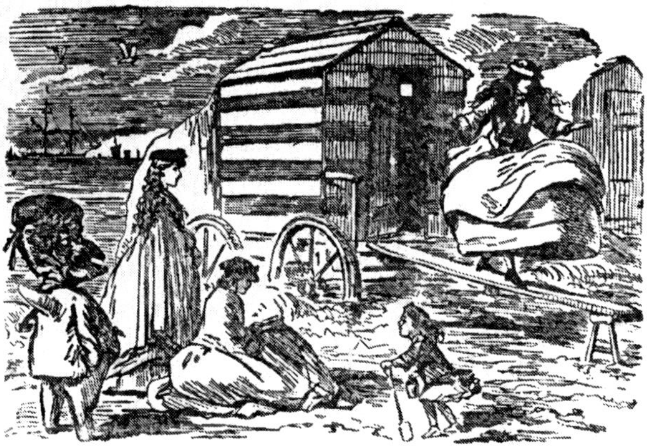

SCENE AT SANDBATH

The Female Blondin Outdone! Grand Morning Performance on the Narrow Plank by the Darling * * * * *

from whom we have expectations, and who is Constance Edith Amelia's Godmother, to come down and stay a week with us?

Shall we be praiseworthily economical, and determine not to spend a single unnecessary sixpence; or shall we, as we *have* come to Pierpoint, enjoy ourselves to the utmost, go in for all the amusements of the place—pier, public gardens, theatre, concerts, Oceanarium, bathing, boating, fishing, driving, riding, and rinking—make excursions, be ostentatiously liberal to the Town

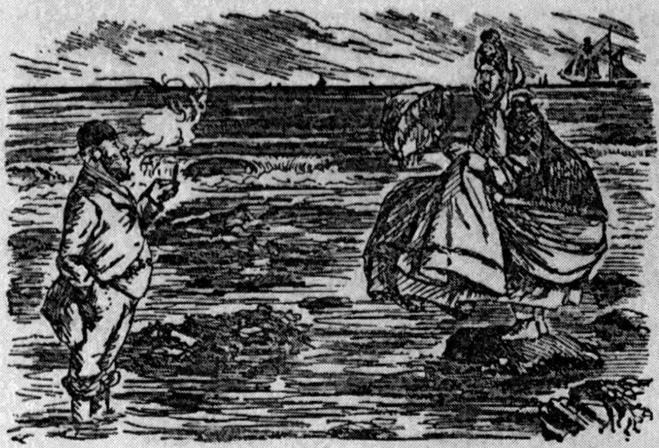

A LITTLE FAMILY BREEZE

Mrs. T. "What a wretch you must be, T.; why don't you take me off? Don't you see I'm overtook with the tide, and I shall be drownded!"

T. "Well, then—will you promise not to kick up such a row when I stop out late of a Saturday?"

Band, and buy everything that is offered to us on the Beach?

A month hence, shall we be glad or sorry to leave Pierpoint, and go back to Paddington?

POSTSCRIPT TO A SEASIDE LETTER.—"The sea is as smooth, and clear, as a looking-glass. The oysters might see to shave in it."

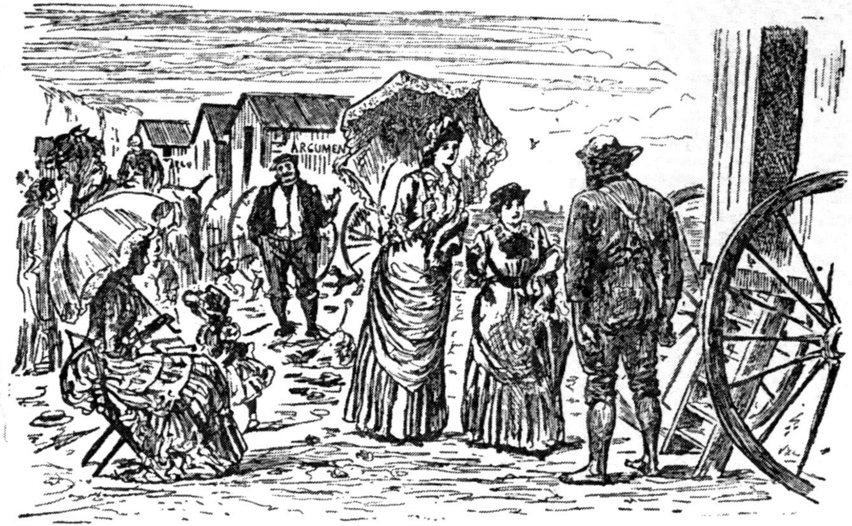

ALL IN THE DAY'S WORK

"And look here! I want you to take my friend here and myself just far enough to be up to our chins, you know, and no further!"

WHAT THE WILD WAVES ARE SAYING

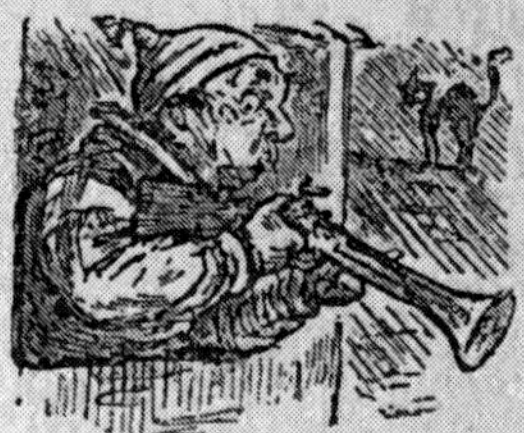

BANGOR

THAT the lodging-house keepers are on the look out for the weary Londoners and their boxes.

That the sea breezes will attract all the world from the Metropolis to the coast.

That Britons should prefer Ramsgate, Eastbourne, Scarborough, and the like, to Dieppe, Dinard, and Boulogne.

That paterfamilias should remember, when paying the bill, that a two months' letting barely compensates for an empty house during the remainder of the year.

That the shore is a place of recreation for all but the bathing-machine horse.

That the circulating libraries are stocked with superfluous copies of unknown novels waiting to be read.

That, finally, during the excursion season, 'Arry will have to be tolerated, if not exactly loved.

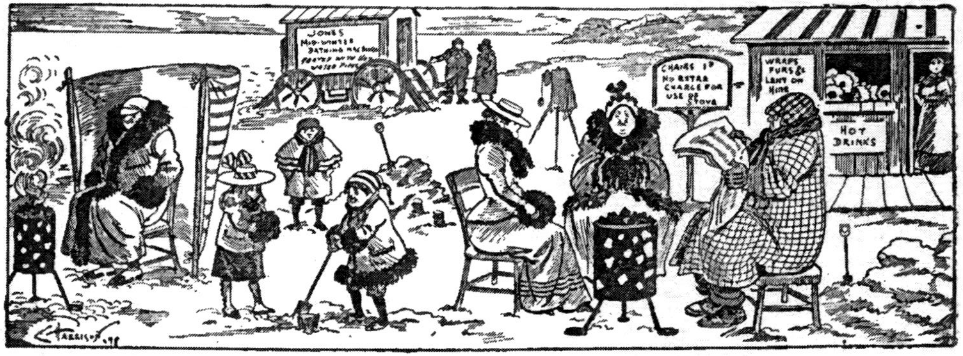

[*The "Lancet" advocates taking holidays in Midwinter instead of Midsummer.*]

View of the sands of Anywhere-on-Sea if the suggestion is adopted.
Time—December or January.

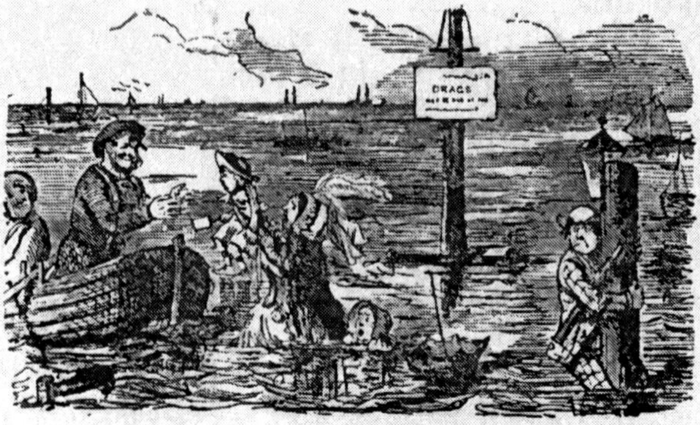

Mrs. Fydgetts (*screaming*). "My child! My child!"

Mr. Fydgetts. "What's the use of making that noise? Can't you be quiet?"

Mrs. F. "You're a brute, sir."

Mr. F. "I wish I were; for then I should be able to swim."

Mrs. F. "Mr. Fydgetts! Ain't you a-coming to help me?"

Mr. F. "No! It serves you right for bringing me down to this stupid place."

Mrs. F. "*I*, indeed. Why, I wanted to go to Brighton and you would come to Margate—You said it was cheaper."

Mr. F. "It's false; I said no such thing."

Mrs. F. "You did, you did!"

Mr. F. "O, woman! woman! Where do you expect to go to?"

Mrs. F. "To the bottom; unless you come and help me!"

Mr. F. "Help yourself. I'm s-i-n-k-i-n-g"—

Mrs. F. "My child! My child!"

Mr. F. (*rising from the water*). "Be quiet, can't you! Woo-o-m—" (*the rest is inaudible, but the watery pair are saved just in time, and renew their dispute in the boat as soon as they are rescued from their perilous position*).

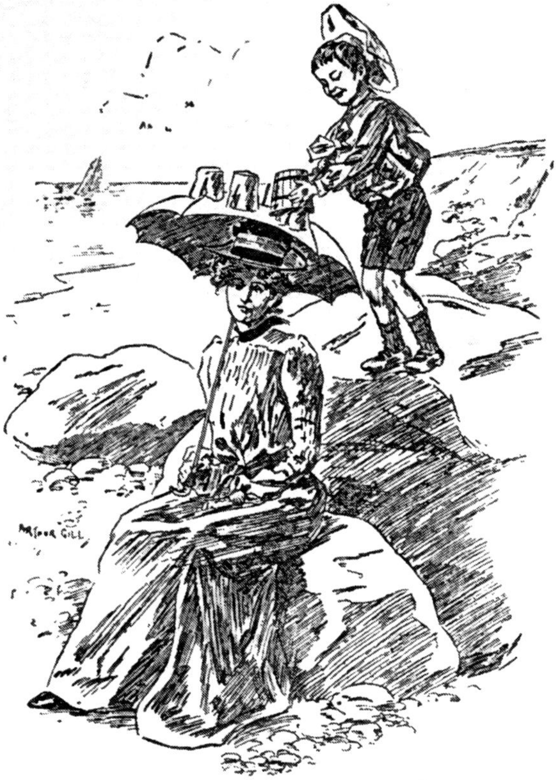

Mabel (*soliloquising*). "Dear me, this relaxing climate makes even one's parasol seem too heavy to hold!"

HOLIDAY HAUNTS

By Jingle Junior on the Jaunt

I.—GREAT YARMOUTH

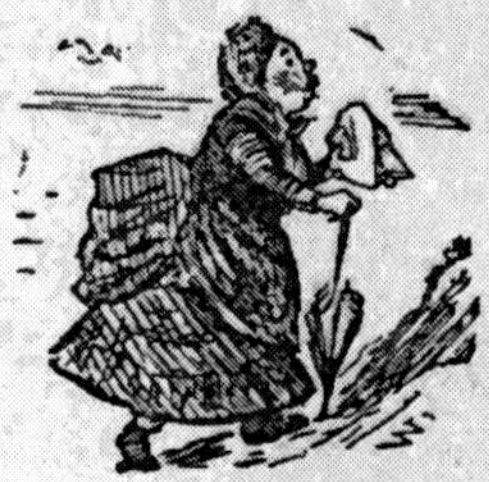

PUFFINS

WHY Great?—where's Little Yarmouth?—or Mid-Sized Yarmouth?—give it up — don't know — hate people who ask conundrums —feel well cured directly you get here—good trade-mark for dried-fish sellers, "The Perfect Cure"—if you stay a fortnight, get quite kipperish—stay a month, talk kipperish! Principal attractions—Bloaters and Rows — first eat—second see—song, "*Speak gently of the Herring*"—"long shore" ones splendid — kippers delicious—song, "*What's a' the steer, Kipper?*" —song, "*Nobody's rows like our Rows*"—more they are — varied — picturesque — tumbledown — paradise for painters — very narrow — capital support for native Bloater going home after dinner —odd names—Ramp, Kitty Witches—Gallon Can,

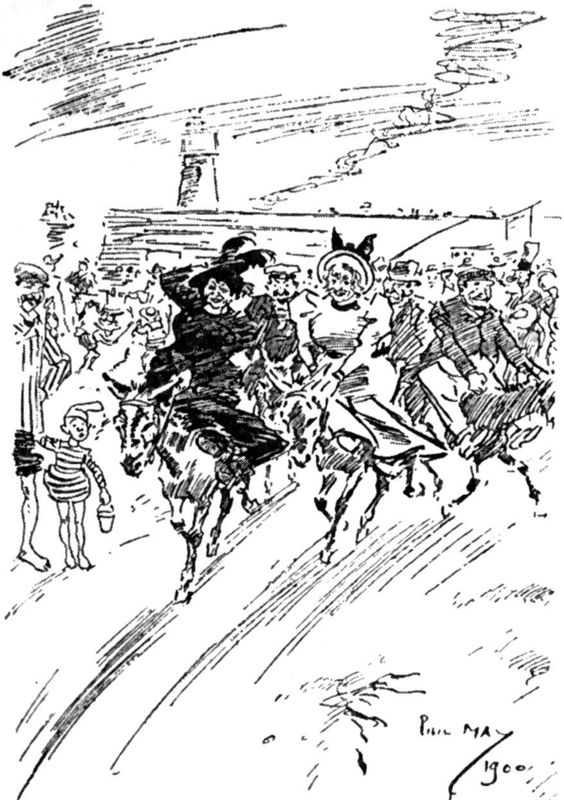

THE DONKEYS' HOLIDAY

With compliments to the S.P.C.A.

Conge! Fancy oneself quite the honest toiler of the sea—ought to go about in dried haddock suit—feel inclined to emulate *Mr. Peggotty*—run into quiet taverns—thump tables violently—say "gormed!" Whole neighbourhood recalls *Ham* and *Little Em'ly* — *David*, *Steerforth*, *Mrs. Gummidge*—recall ham myself—if well broiled—lunch—pleasant promenades on piers—plenty of amusement in watching the bloateric commerce—fresh water fishing in adjacent Broads, if you like—if not, let it alone—broad as it's long! The Denes—not sardines—nor rural deans—good places for exercise—plenty of antiquities—old customs—quaint traditions! Picturesque ancient taverns—capital modern hotels—stopping in one of the latter—polite waiter just appeared — dinner served — soup'll get cold—mustn't wait—never insult good cook by being unpunctual — rather let Editor go short than hurt cook's feelings*—so no more at present—from Yours Truly.

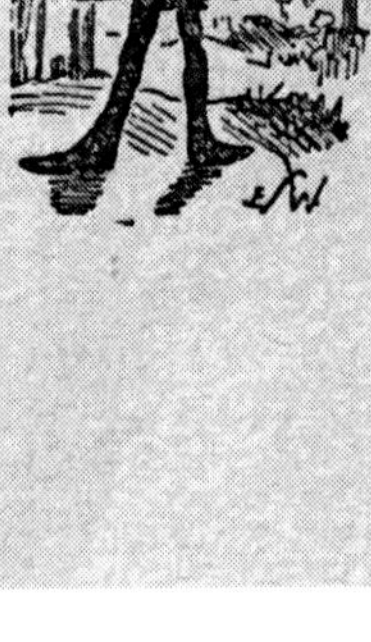

* Don't like this sentiment. Is J. J. a Cook's Tourist?—ED.

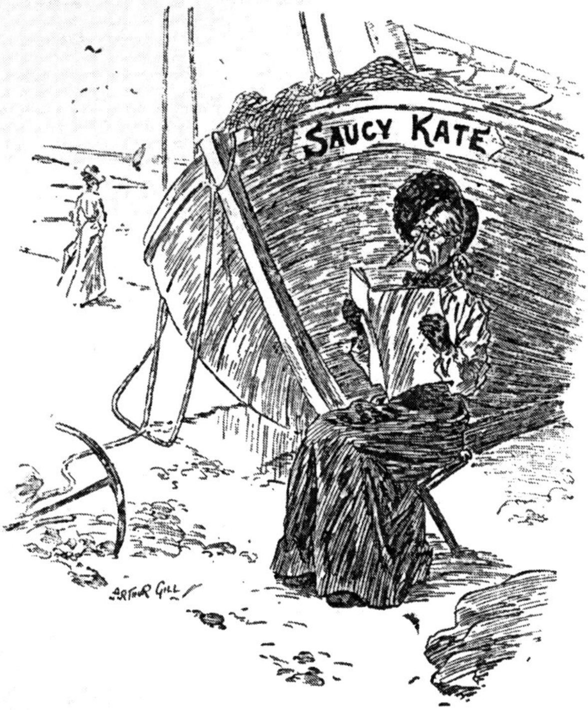

LABELLED!

II.—LITTLEHAMPTON.

EMPHATICALLY the Sea on the strict Q T—no bustle at railway-station—train glides in noiselessly—passengers ooze away—porters good-tempered and easy-going—like suffragan Bishops in corduroys—bless boxes—read pastorals on portmanteaux—no one in a hurry—locomotive coos softly in an undertone—fly-drivers suggest possibility of your requiring their services in a whisper! Place full—no lodgings to be had—visitors manage to efface themselves—no one about—all having early dinners—or gone to bed—or pretending to be somewhere else—a one-sided game of hide and seek—everybody hiding, nobody seeking! Seems always afternoon—dreamy gleamy sunshine—a dense quietude that you might cut in slices—no braying brass-bands—no raucous niggers—no seaside harpies—Honfleur packet only excitement—no one goes to see it start—visitors don't like to be excited! Chief amusements, Common, Sands, and Pony-chaises—first, good to roll on—second, good to stroll on—

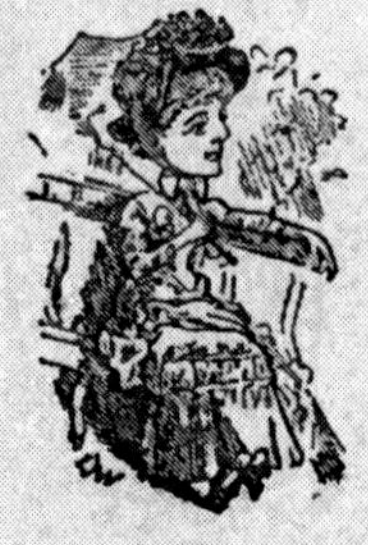

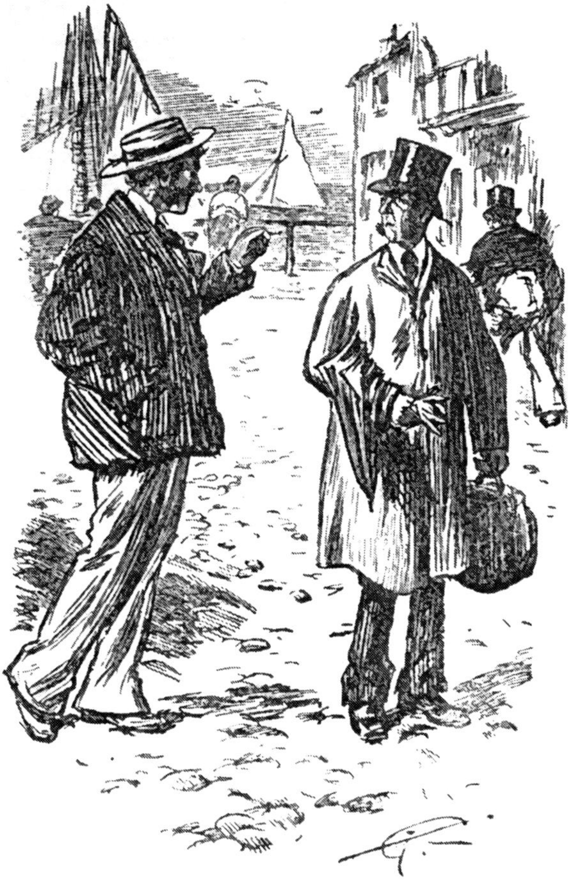

NAUGHTICAL?

Yachting Friend (*playfully*). "Have you any experience of squalls, Brown?"

Brown. "Squalls!" (*Seriously.*) My dear sir, I've brought up ten in family!"

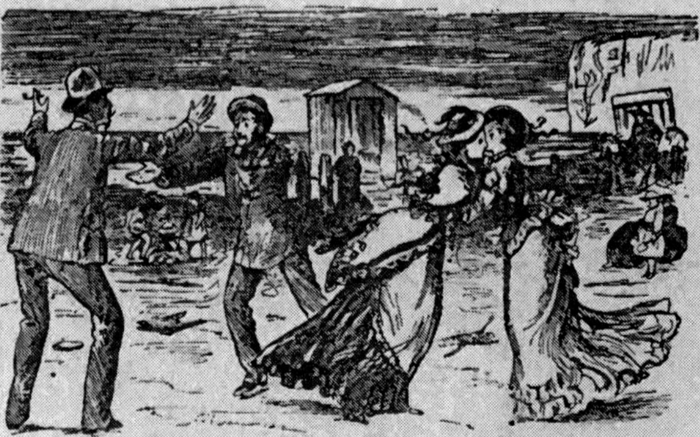

SOCIAL BEINGS

Wearied by London dissipation, the Marjoribanks Browns go, for the sake of perfect quiet, to that picturesque little watering-place, Shrimpington-super-Mare, where they trust that they will not meet a single soul they know.

Oddly enough, the Cholmondeley Joneses go to the same spot with the same purpose.

Now, these Joneses and Browns cordially detest each other in London, and are not even on speaking terms; yet such is the depressing effect of "perfect quiet" that, as soon as they meet at Shrimpington-super-Mare, they rush into each other's arms with a wild sense of relief!

first two, gratuitous and breezy—third, inexpensive and easy—might be driven out of your mind for three-and-six — notwithstanding this, everybody presumably sane. Capital place for children—cricket for boys—shrimping for girls—bare legs—picturesque dress—not much caught—

salt water good for ankles—excellent bathing—rows of bathing-tents—admirable notion! Interesting excursions — Arundel Castle — Bramber — Bognor — Chichester — Petworth House! Good things to eat—Arundel mullet—Amberley trout—Tarring figs! Delightful air—omnipotent ozone—uninterrupted quiet—just the place to recover your balance, either mental or monetary—I wish to

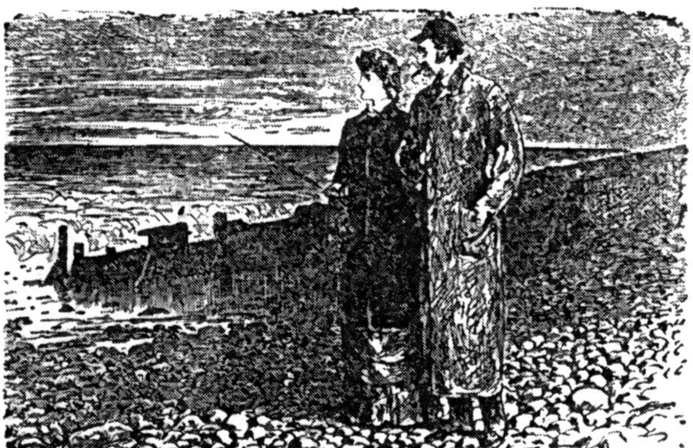

HEARTS OF OAK

Angelina (who has never seen a revolving light before). "How patient and persevering those sailors must be, Edwin! The wind has blown that light out six times since they first lit it, and they've lighted it again each time!"

RAMSGATE

recover both—that's the reason I'm here — send cheque at once to complete cure.*

III.—SCARBOROUGH.

LONG way from London —no matter—fast train—soon here — once here don't wish to leave — palatial hotels—every luxury—good *tables d'hôte*—pleasant balls—lively society! Exhilarating air—good as champagne without "morning after"—up early—go to bed late—authorities provide something better than a broken-down pier, a circulating library, and a rickety bathing-machine —authorities disburse large sums for benefit of visitors—visitors spend lots of money in town—mutual satisfaction—place crowded—capital bands —excellent theatricals—varied entertainments—right way to do it! The Spa—first discovered 1620—people been discovering it ever since—some

* We have sent him the price of a third-class fare to town, with orders to return instantly: possibly this is hardly the sort of check that our friend "J. J." expected.—ED.

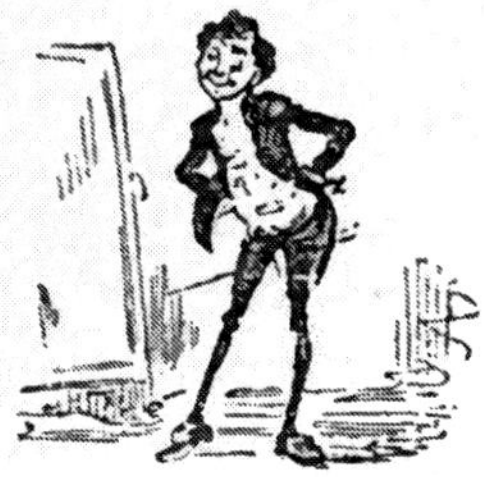

SHANKLIN

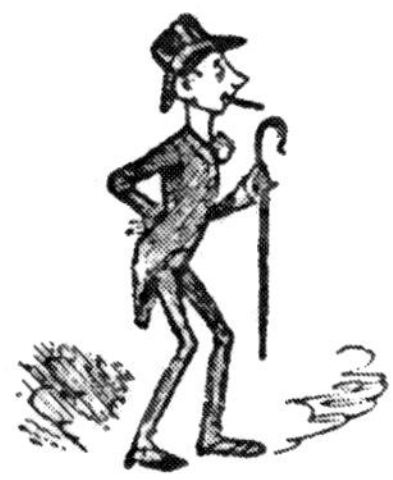

SCILLY

drink it—more walk on it—lounge on it—smoke on it—flirt on it—wonderful costumes in the morning—more wonderful in the afternoon—most wonderful in the evening! North Sands—South Sands—fine old Castle well placed—picturesque old town—well-built modern terraces, squares and streets—pony-chaises—riding-horses—Lift for lazy ones! Capital excursions — Oliver's Mount — Carnelian Bay—Scalby Mill—Hackness—Wykeham—Filey! Delightful gardens—secluded seats

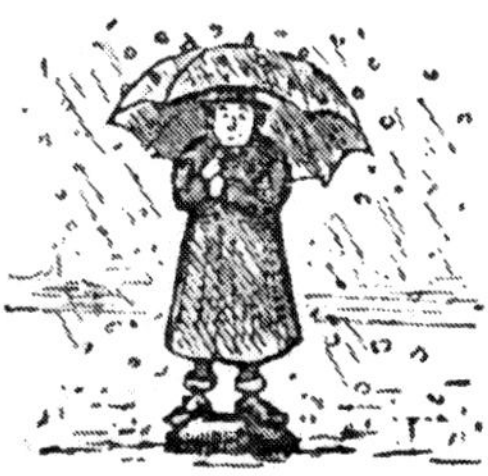

HAYLING ISLAND

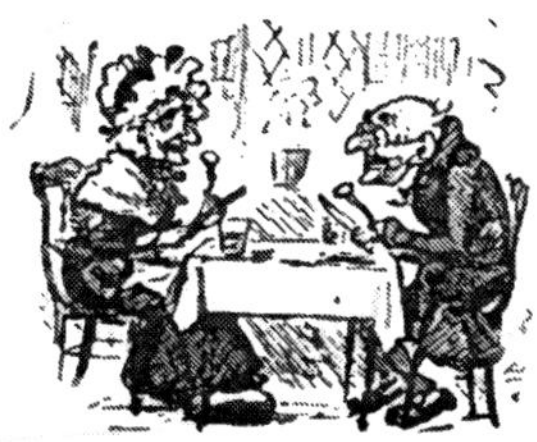

MUMBLES

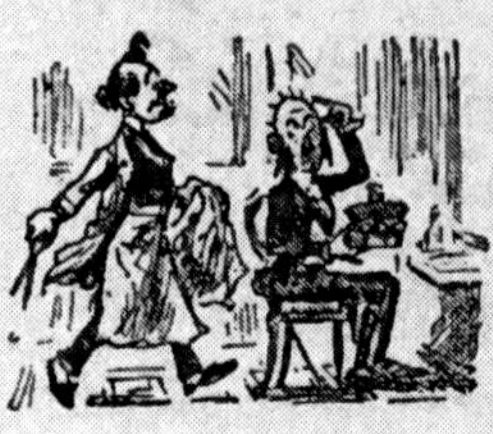

A CUTTER MAKING FOR THE PEER HEAD

—hidden nooks—shady bowers — well - screened corners — Northern Belles — bright eyes—soft nothings — eloquent sighs — squozen hands—before you know where you are—ask papa—all up — dangerous very! Overcome by feelings—can't write any more—friend asks me to drink waters—query North Chalybeate or South Salt Well—wonder which—if in doubt try soda qualified with brandy —good people scarce—better run no risk!

COSTUME IN KEEPING.—"Of all sweet things," said Bertha, "for the seaside, give me a serge." The Ancient Mariner shook his head. He didn't see the joke.

BOARD AND LODGING!—*Landlady.* "Yes, sir, the board were certingly to be a guinea a week, but I didn't know as you was a-going to bathe in the sea before breakfast and take bottles of tonic during the day!"

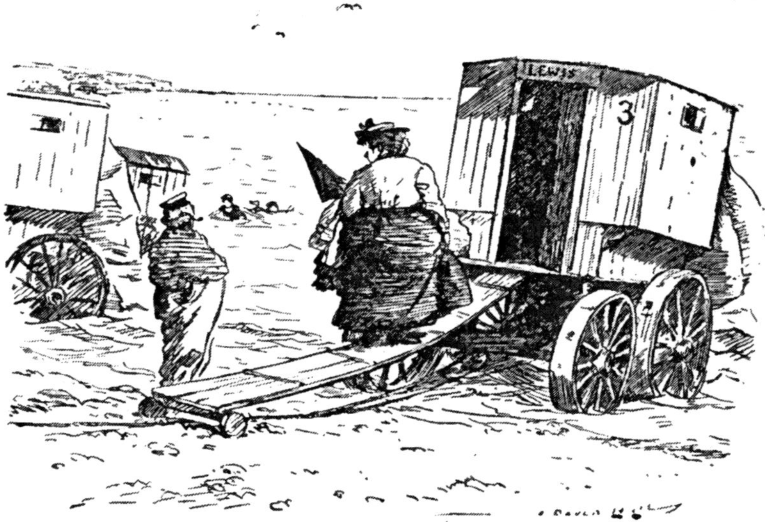

" Now, mind, if any of those nasty people with cameras come near, you're to send them away ! "

SEASIDE SOLITUDE

HIGHBURYBARN-ON-SEA

(From our Special Commissioner)

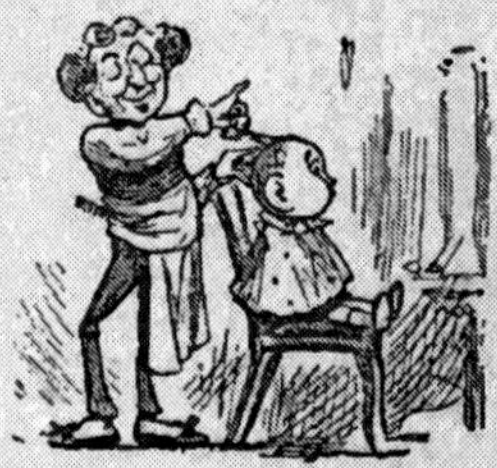

A CUTTER ROUNDING THE BUOY

DEAR MR. PUNCH,—This is a spot, which, according to your instructions, I reached last evening. In these same instructions you described it as "a growing place." I fancy it must be of the asparagus order, that vegetable, as you are well aware, taking three years in which to develop itself to perfection. Highburybarn-on-Sea is, I regret to say, in the first stage—judged from an asparagus point of view. I cannot entertain the enthusiastic description of the candid correspondent. (I refer to the cutting forwarded by you from an eminent daily paper under the heading, "By the Golden Ocean.") He describes it as "an oasis on the desert coast of Great Britain."

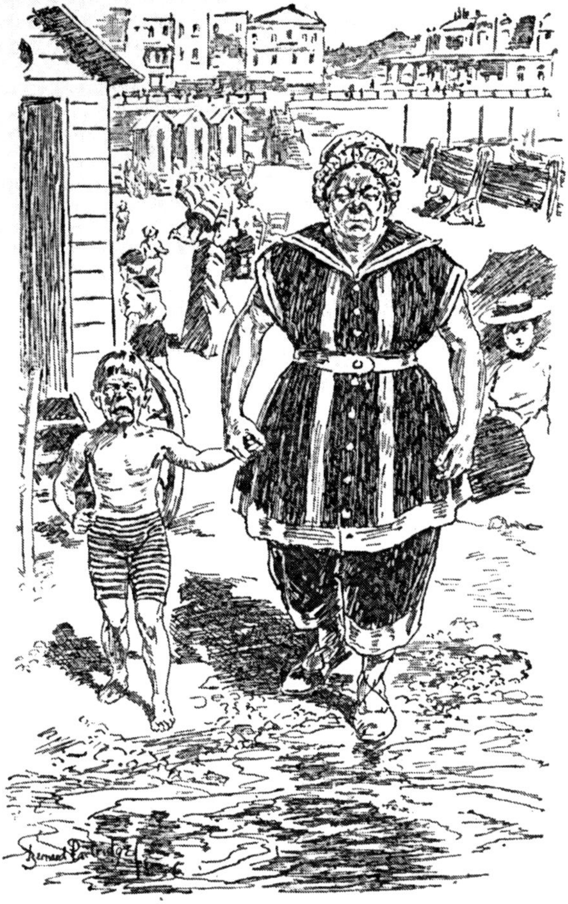

THE BATHING QUESTION

Master Tommy is emphatically of the opinion that the sexes ought not to bathe together.

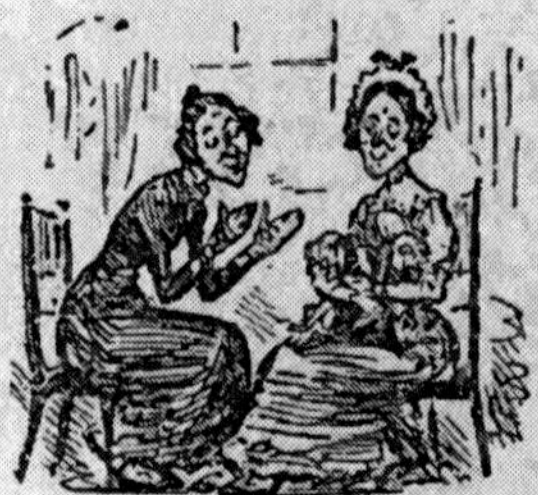

LIMPETS

Far be it from me to deny the desert—all I object to is the oasis.

I ask you, sir, if you ever, in the course of the travels in which you have out-rivalled Stanley, Cameron, Livingstone, Harry de Windt, and, may I add, De Rougemont, ever came across an oasis, consisting of two score villas, built with scarcely baked bricks, reposing on an arid waste amid a number of tumbled-down cottages, and surmounted by a mighty workhouse-like hotel looking down on a pre-Adamite beershop?

The sky was blue, the air was fresh, the waves had retreated to sea when I arrived in a jolting omnibus at Highburybarn-on-Sea, and deposited myself and luggage at the Metropolitan Hotel. A page-boy was playing airs on a Jew's-harp when I alighted on the sand-driven steps of the hostelry. He seemed surprised at my arrival, but in most respectful fashion placed his organ of minstrelsy in his jacket pocket, the while he conveyed my Gladstone

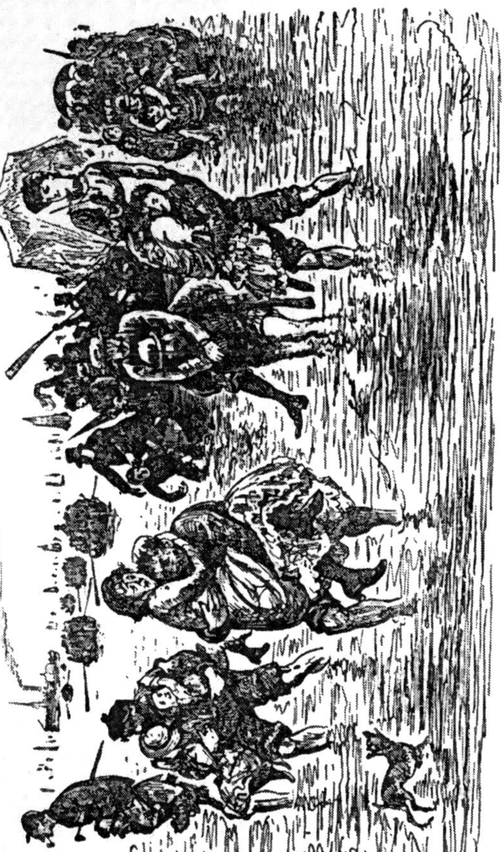

WHITBOROUGH. LOW TIDE. ARRIVAL OF THE SCARBY STEAMER

TAKING A DIP AND GETTING A BLOW

bag to my apartment, secured by an interview with an elderly dame, who gave an intelligent but very wan smile when I suggested dinner. She referred me to the head waiter. This functionary pointed in grandiose fashion to the coffee-room, wherein some artistic wall-papering wag had committed atrocities on which it would be libel to comment.

There was only one occupant, a short clean-shaven gentleman with white hair and a red nose, who was apparently chasing space. This turned out to be a militant blue-bottle. Meantime, the head-waiter produced his bill of fare, or rather the remains of it. Nearly every dish had apparently been consumed, for the most tempting *plats* were removed from the *menu* by a liberal application of red pencil. Finally, I decided on a fried sole and a steak. The white-haired man still pursued the blue-bottle.

I went up to my room, and after washing with no

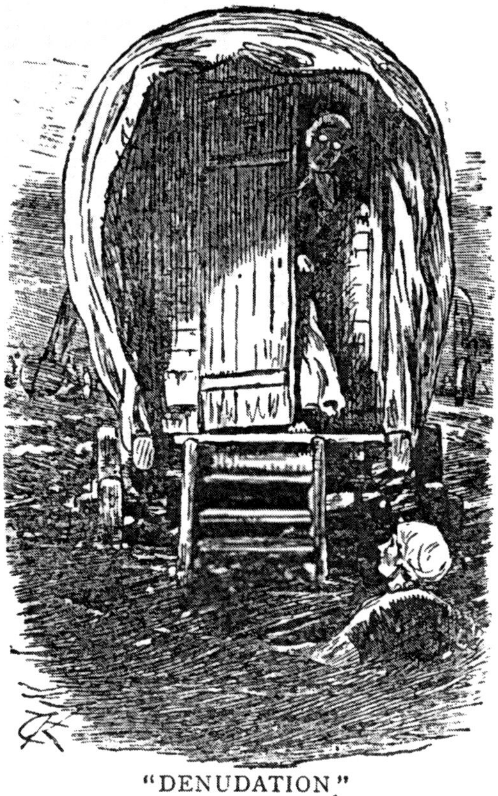

"DENUDATION."

Niece (after a header). "Oh, aunt, you're not coming in with your spectacles on?"

Aunt Clarissa (who is not used to bathe in the "open"). "My dear, I positively won't take off anything more, I'm determined!!"

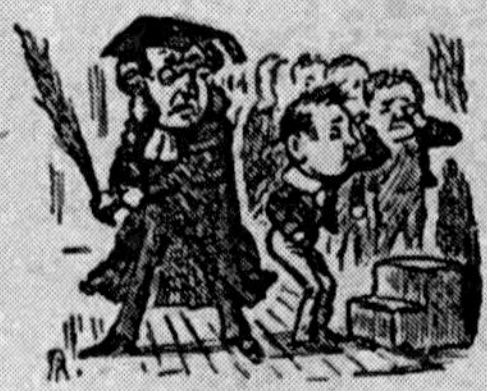
BIRCHINGTON

soap I returned to the coffee-room. The blue-bottle still had the best of it. The head-waiter, after the lapse of an hour, informed me that the sole would not be long. When it arrived, I found that he spoke the truth. If you have any recollection of the repast which *Porthos* endured when entertained by *Madame Coquenard*, you will have some notion of my feast. The head-waiter told me that some bare-legged persons who had waded into the water were shrimp-catchers. I only wished that I were one of them, for at least they found food.

Later on I retired to rest. I was visited in the hours of darkness, to which I had consigned myself, by a horde of mosquitoes, imported, so I was informed in the morning, by American travellers, who never tipped the waiters. I fulfilled their obligations, still gazing on the auburn sand-drift, still looking on the sea, still feeling hungry and murmuring to myself, "Highburybarn-on-Sea would be a capital place for children, if I could only see any cows." A melancholy cocoa-nut shy by the station appeared to afford all the milk in the place.

Yours despondently,

NIBBLETHORPE NOBBS.

EMBARRASSMENT OF RICHES: MARGATE.—*Mother.* "Now, Tommy, which would you rather do—have a donkey ride or watch father bathe?"

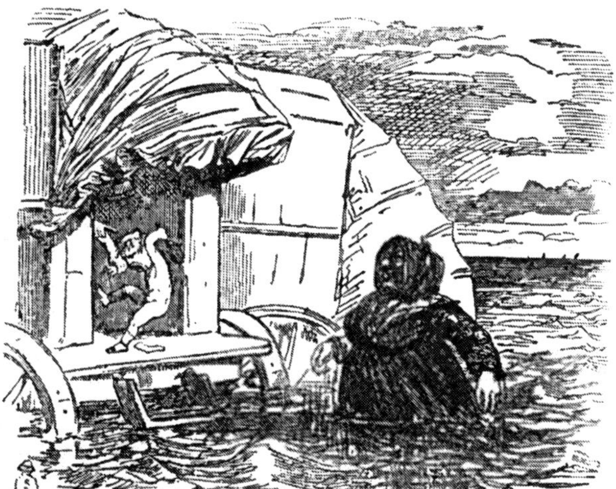

Bathing Woman. "Master Franky wouldn't cry! No! Not he!—He'll come to his Martha, and bathe like a man!"

TO THE FIRST BATHING-MACHINE

(*After Wordsworth*)

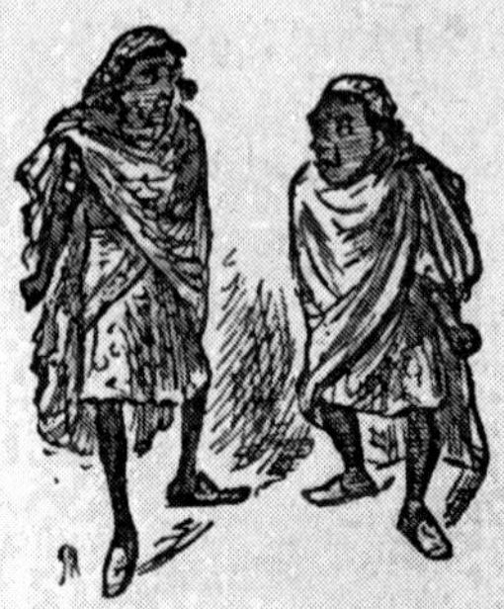

MOORINGS

O BLANK new-comer! I have seen,
I see thee with a start:
So gentle looking a Machine,
Infernal one thou art!

When first the sun feels rather hot,
Or even rather warm,
From some dim, hibernating spot
Rolls forth thy clumsy form.

Perhaps thou babblest to the sea
Of sunshine and of flowers;
Thou bringest but a thought to me
Of such bad quarter hours.

I, grasping tightly, pale with fear,
Thy very narrow bench,
Thou, bounding on in wild career,
All shake, and jolt, and wrench.

Till comes an unexpected stop;
My forehead hits the door,
And I, with cataclysmic flop,
Lie on thy sandy floor.

Then, dressed in Nature's simplest style,
I, blushing, venture out;
And find the sea is still a mile
Away, or thereabout.

Blithe little children on the sand
  Laugh out with childish glee;
Their nurses, sitting near at hand,
  All giggling, stare at me.

Unnerved, unwashed, I rush again
  Within thy tranquil shade,
And wait until the rising main
  Shall banish child and maid.

Thy doors I dare not open now,
  Thy windows give no view;
'Tis late; I will not bathe, I vow:
  I dress myself anew.

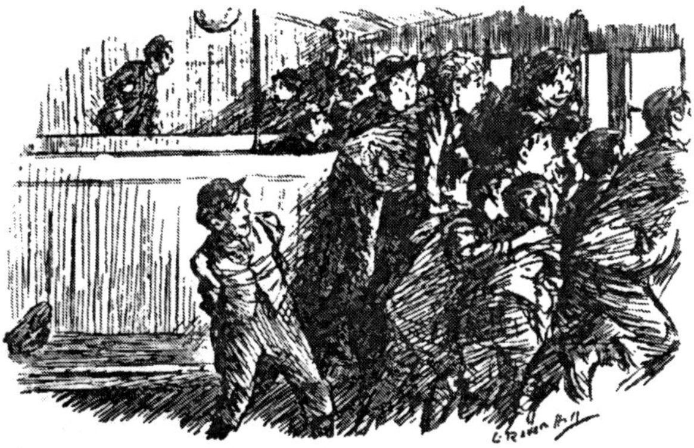

"THALATTA! THALATTA!"

General chorus (*as the children's excursion nears its destination*). "Oh, I say! There's the sea! 'Ooray!!"
Small boy. "I'll be in fust!"

HOW TO ENJOY A HOLIDAY

A Social Contrast

I.—The Wrong Way

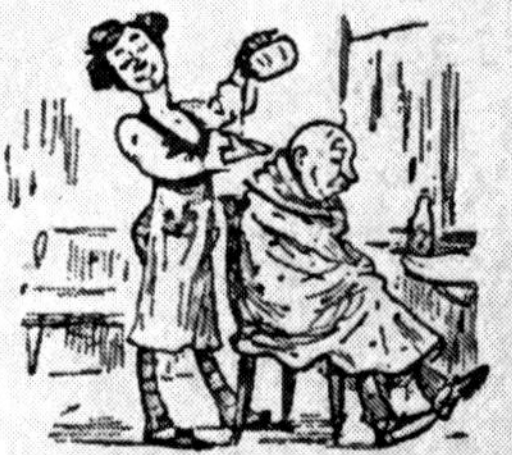

ILE OF MAN

Pater. Here at last! A nice reward for a long and tedious journey!

Mater. Well, you were always complaining in town.

Pater. Broken chairs, rickety table, and a hideous wall-paper!

Mater. Well, I didn't buy the chairs, make the table, or choose the wall-paper. Discontent is your strong point.

Pater. And is likely to remain so. Really, that German band is unbearable!

Mater. My dear, you have no ear for music. Why, you don't even care for my songs! You used to say you liked them once.

Pater. So I did—thirty years ago!

Mater. Before our marriage! And I have survived thirty years!

Pater. Eh? What do you mean by that, madam?

Mater. Anything you please. But come—dinner's ready.

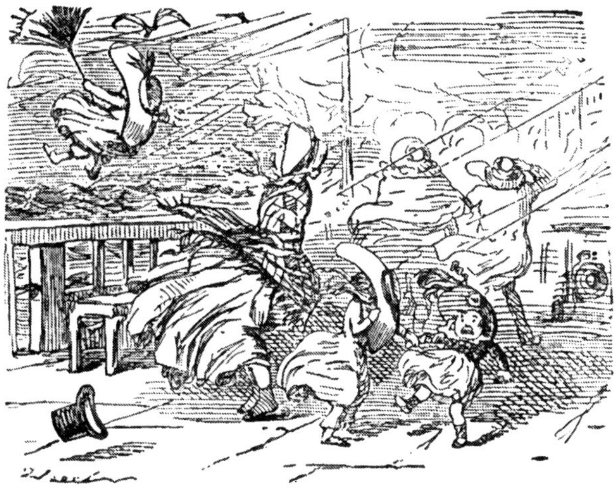

AWFUL SCENE ON THE CHAIN PIER, BRIGHTON

Nursemaid. "Lawk! There goes Charley, and he's took his mar's parasol. What *will* missus say?"

Pater. Dinner! The usual thing, I suppose—underdone fish and overdone meat!

Mater. Well, I see that you are determined to make the best of everything, my dear!

Pater. I am glad you think so, my darling!

[*And so they sit down to dinner.*

II.—The Right Way.

Pater. Here at last! What a charming spot! A fitting sequel to a very pleasant journey!

Mater. And yet you are very fond of town!

Pater. This room reminds me of my own cozy study. Venerable chairs, a strange old table, and a quaintly-designed wall-paper.

Mater. Well, I think if I had had to furnish the house, I should have chosen the same things myself. But had they been ever so ugly, I feel sure that you would have liked them. You know, sir, that content is your strong point.

Pater. I am sure that I shall find no opportunity of getting any merit (after the fashion of *Mark Tapley*) for being contented in this pleasant spot. What a capital German band!

Mater. I don't believe that you understand

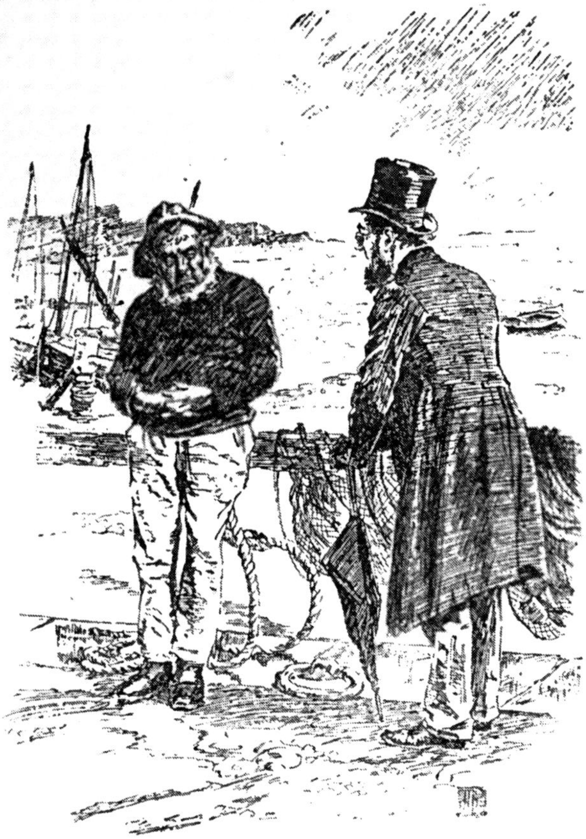

Temperance Enthusiast. "Look at the beautiful lives our first parents led. Do you suppose *they* ever gave way to strong drink?"

The Reprobate. "I 'xpect Eve must 'a' done. She saw snakes!"

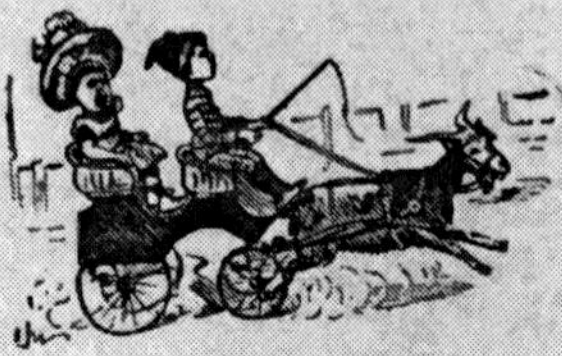

A GOAT AND TWO KIDS

anything about music, sir. Why, you even pretend that you like my old songs!

Pater. And so I do. Every day I live I like them better and better. And yet I heard them for the first time thirty years ago!

Mater. When we were married! And so I have survived thirty years!

Pater. Eh? What do you mean by that, madam?

Mater. That I am a living proof that kindness never kills. How happy we have been! But come—dinner's ready.

Pater. Dinner! The usual thing, I suppose—a nice piece of fish and a juicy joint. Now, that's just what I like. So much better than our pretentious London dinners! Not that a London dinner is not very good in its proper place.

Mater. Well, I see that you are determined to make the best of everything, my dear.

Pater. I am glad you think so, my darling!

[*And so* they *sit down to dinner.*

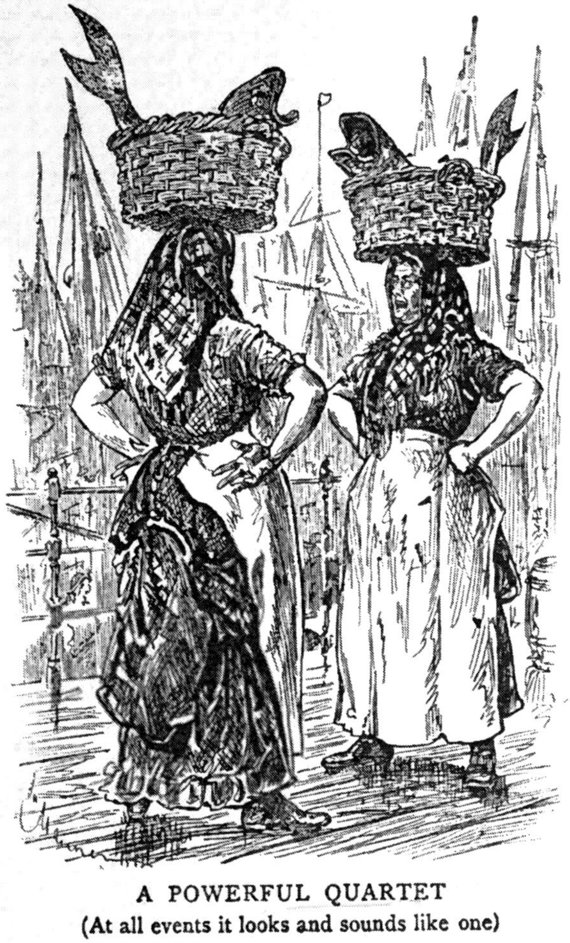

A POWERFUL QUARTET
(At all events it looks and sounds like one)

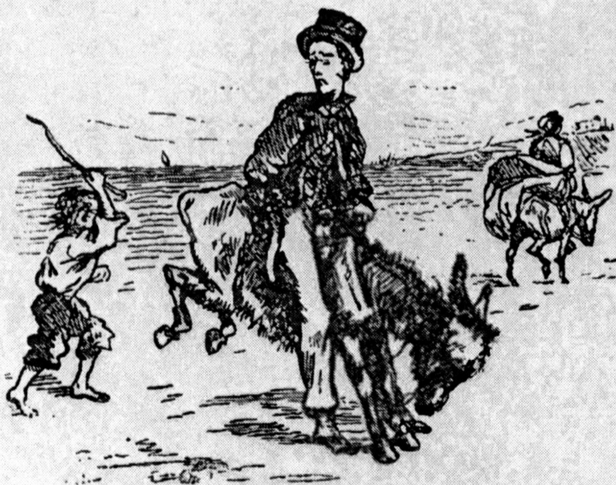

SWEETS OF THE SEASIDE

Shingleton, near Dulborough.

SYMPATHISING MR. PUNCH,

With the desire of enjoying a few days of tranquillity and a few dips in the sea, I have arrived and taken lodgings at this "salubrious watering-place" (as the guide-books choose to call it), having heard that it was quiet, and possessed of a steep, cleanly, and bathe-inviting beach. As to the latter point, I find that fame has not belied it; but surely with a view to tempt me into suicide, some demon must have coupled the term "quiet" with this place. Quiet! Gracious Powers of Darkness! if this be your idea of a quiet spot to live in, I wonder what, according to your notion, need be added to its tumult to make a noisy town. Here is a list of aural tortures wherewith we are tormented, which may serve by way of time-table to advertise the musical attractions of the place:—

1 A.M.—Voices of the night. Revellers returning home.

1.30 A.M.—Duet, "*Io t'amo*," squealed upon the tiles, by the famous feline vocalists Mademoiselle Minette and Signor Catterwaulini.

2 A.M.—Barc-arole and chorus, "*Bow wow wow*" (BACH), by the Bayers of the Moon.

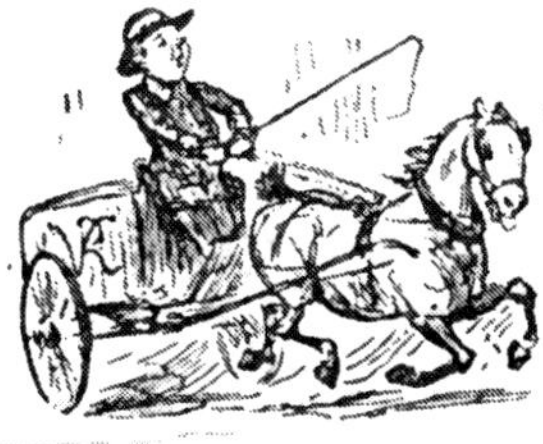

REDCAR

3 A.M.—Song without words, by the early village cock.

3.30 A.M.—Chorus by his neighbours, high and low, mingling the treble

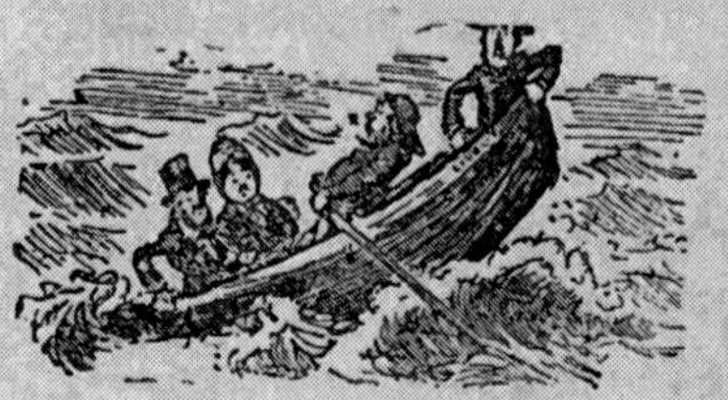
ENJOYING THE HEIGHT OF THE SEAS-ON

of the Bantam with the Brahma's thorough bass.

4 A.M. — Twittering of swallows, and chirping of early birds, before they go to catch their worms.

4.45 A.M.—Meeting of two natives, of course *just* under your window, who converse in a stage-whisper at the tip-top of their voices.

5 A.M.—Stampede of fishermen, returning from their night's work in their heavy boots.

6 A.M.—Start of shrimpers, barefooted, but occasionally bawling.

7 A.M.—Shutters taken down, and small boys sally forth and shout to one another from the two ends of the street.

7.15 A.M.—" So-holes! fine fresh so-holes!"

7.30 A.M.—" Mack'reel! fower a shillun! Ma-a-ack'reel!"

8 A.M.—Piano play begins, and goes on until midnight.

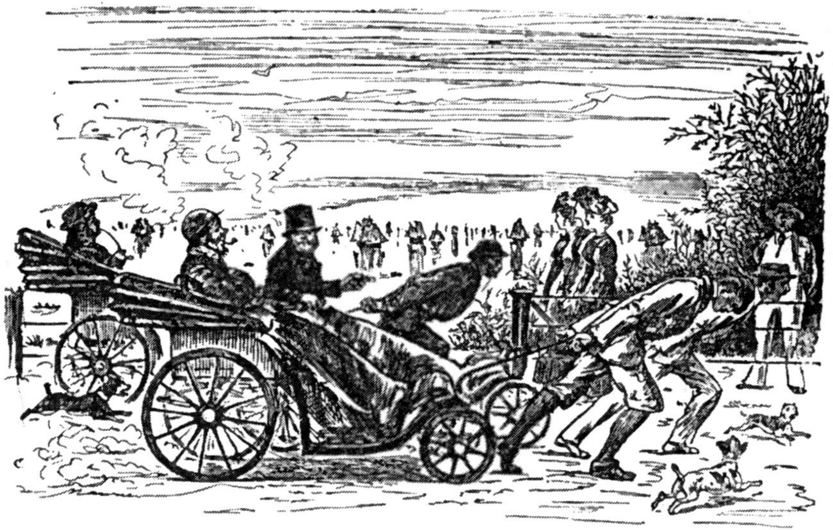

HOW TO KILL TIME AT THE SEASIDE

Hire bath-chairs, put the bath-chairmen inside, and drag them as fast as you can up and down the parade.

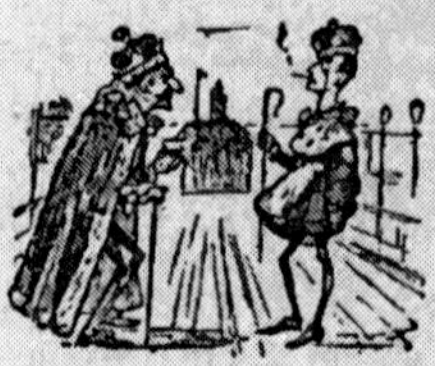

MEETING OF THE OLD AND NEW PEERS AT BRIGHTON

8.25 A.M.—Barrel-organ at the corner. Banjo in the distance.

9 A.M.—German band to right of you. Ophicleide out of time, clarionette out of tune.

9.30 A.M.—"Pa-aper, mornin' pa-aper! *Daily Telegraft!*"

9.45 A.M.—German band to left of you. Clarionette and cornet both out of time and tune.

10.15 A.M.—A key-bugler and a bag-piper a dozen yards apart.

11 A.M.—Performance of Punch and Toby, who barks more than is good for him.

11.30 A.M.—Bellowing black-faced ballad-bawlers, with their banjoes and their bones.

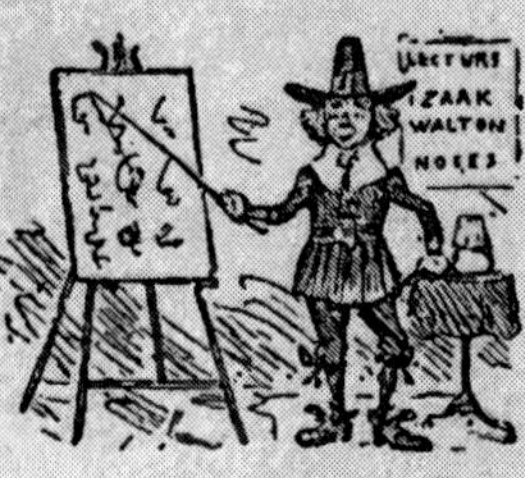

WALTON ON THE NAZE

Such is our daily programme of music until noon, and such, with sundry variations, it continues until midnight. Small wonder that I have so little relish for my meals,

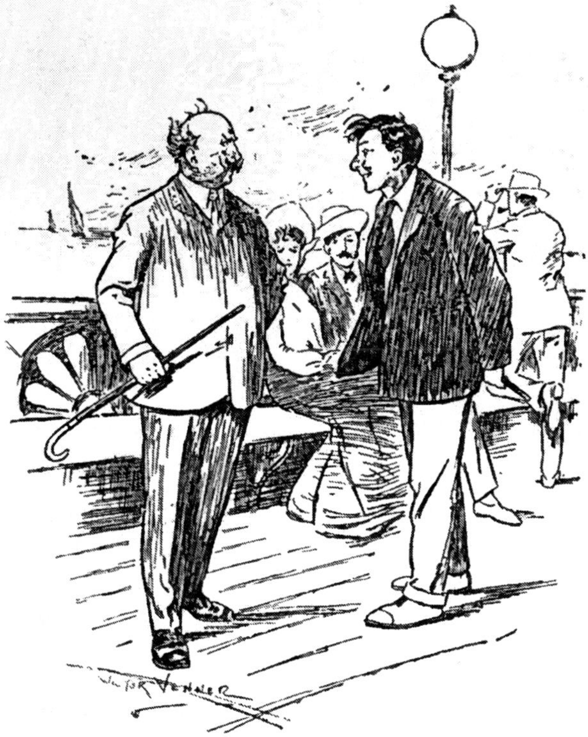

INOPPORTUNE

Enthusiast of the "No Hat Brigade" (to elderly gentleman, who has just lost his hat). "Fine idea this, sir, for the hair, eh?"

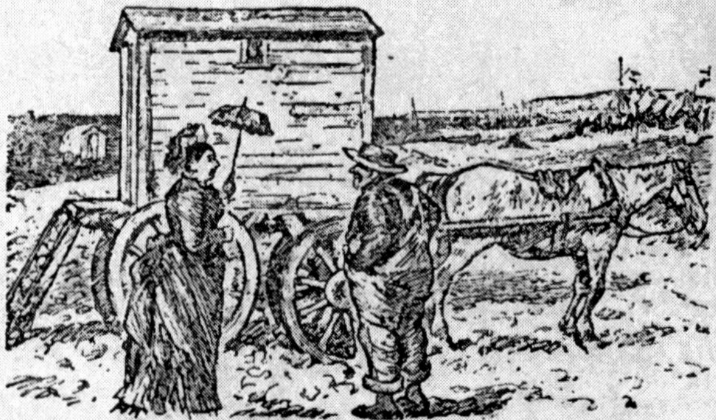

"THE MEAT SUPPLY"

Bathing-man. "Yes, mum, he's a good old 'orse yet. And he's been in the salt water so long, he'll make capital biled beef when we're done with him ! ! !"

and that, in spite of the sea air, I can hardly sleep a wink. I shall return to Town to-morrow, for surely all the street tormentors must be out of it, judging by the numbers that now plague the sad seaside.

MISERRIMUS.

Our Poetess. "Do not talk to me of dinner, Edwin. I must stay by this beautiful Sea, and *drink it all in!*"

Bill the Boatman. "Lor! She's a thirsty one too!"

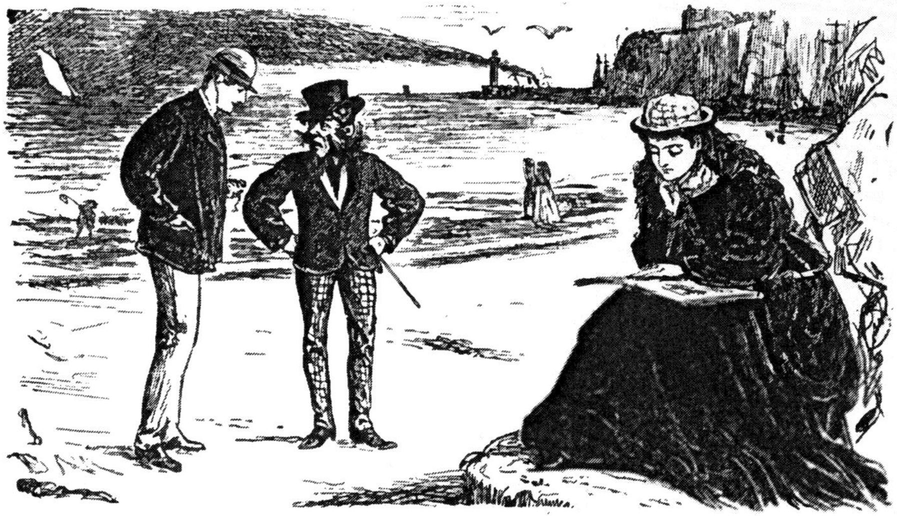

Jones. "Hullo, Brown, what's the matter with you and Mrs. Brown?"

Brown. "Matter? Why, do you know what they call us down here? They call us Beauty and the Beast! Now I should like to know what my poor wife has done to get such a name as that!"

THE TREACHEROUS TIDE

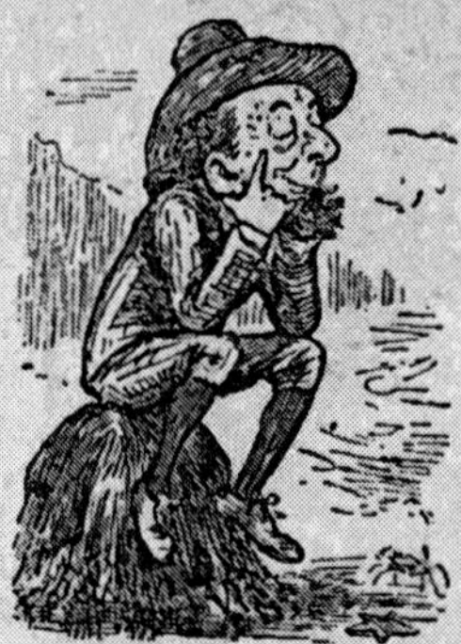

I SAT on a slippery rock,
  In the grey cliff's opal shade,
And the wanton waves went curvetting by
  Like a roystering cavalcade.
And they doffed their crested plumes,
  As they kissed the blushing sand,
Till her rosy face dimpled over with smiles
  At the tricks of the frolicsome band.

Then the kittywake laughed, "Ha! ha!"
  And the sea-mew wailed with pain,
As she sailed away on the shivering wind
  To her home o'er the surging main.
And the jelly-fish quivered with rage,
  While the dog-crabs stood by to gaze,
And the star-fish spread all her fingers abroad,
  And sighed for her grandmothers' days.

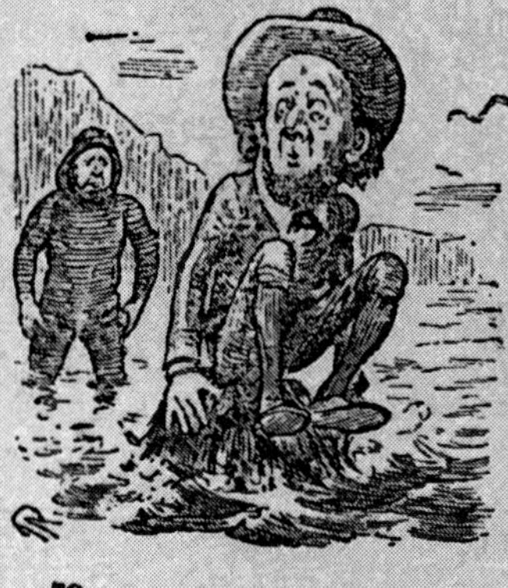

And the curlew screamed,
"Fie! fie!"
And the great gull groaned
at the sight,
And the albatross rose and
fled with a shriek
To her nest on the peril-
ous height.

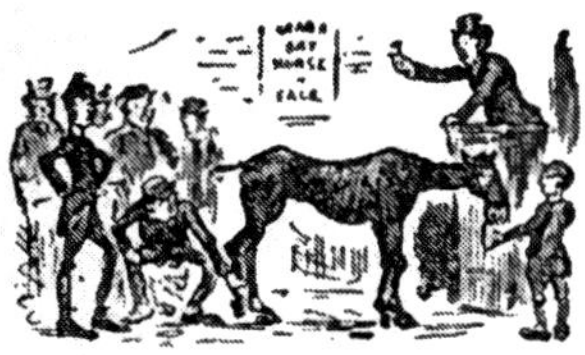

A SAIL OVER THE BAY

* * *

Good gracious! the place where I sat
With sea-water was rapidly filling,
And a hoarse voice cried, "Sir, you're caught by the tide!
And I'll carry ye off for a shilling!"

"LOCAL COLOUR."—PLACE: South Parade, Cheapenham-on-Sea.—*Edith.* "Mabel dear, would you get me *Baedeker's Switzerland* and the last Number of the *World.*"

Mabel. "What do you want *them* for?"

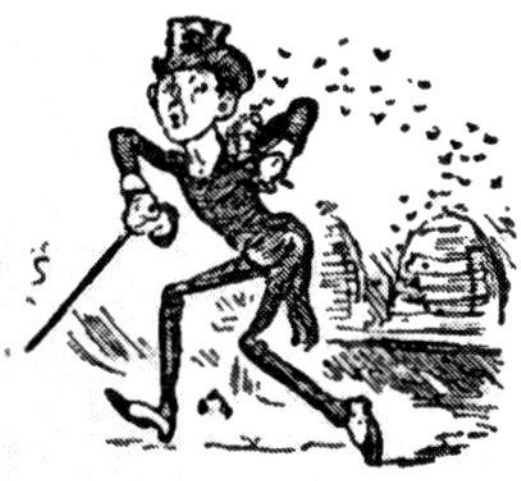

SCENT BEES

Edith. "Oh, I'm writing letters, and we're in the Engadine, you know, and I just want to describe some of our favourite haunts, and mention a few of the people who are staying there—here, I mean."

THE LAY OF THE LAST LODGER

I.

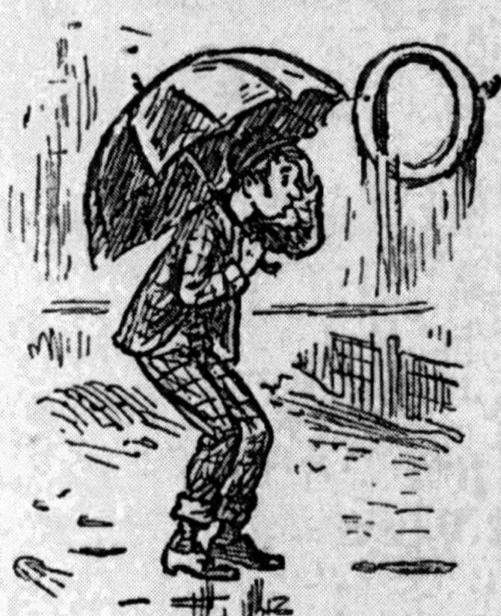

OH dreary, dreary, dreary
me!
My jaw is sore with
yawning—
I'm weary of the dreary
sea,
With its roaring beach
Where sea-gulls screech,
And shrimpers shrimp,
And limpets limp,
And winkles wink,
And trousers shrink;
And the groaning, moaning, droning tide
Goes splashing and dashing from side
to side,
With all its might, from morn to night,
And from night to morning's dawning.

II.

The shore's a flood of puddly mud,
And the rocks are limy and slimy—
And I've tumbled down with a thud—good lud!—
And I fear I swore,
For something tore;
And my shoes are full
Of the stagnant pool;

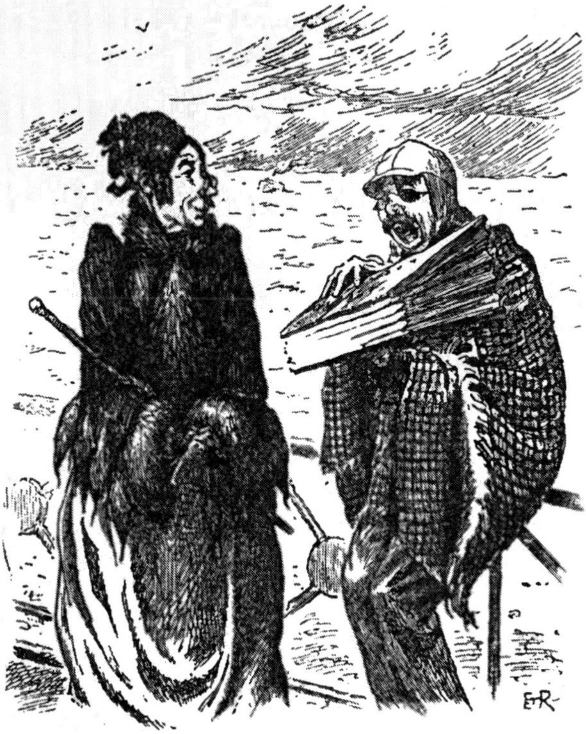

A STARTLING PROPOSITION

Seedy Individual (*suddenly and with startling vigour*)—

"Aoh ! Floy with me ercross ther sea,
Ercross ther dork lergoon ! !"

And hauling, sprawling, crawling crabs
Have got in my socks with starfish and dabs ;
And my pockets are swarming with polypes and prawns,
And noisome beasts with shells and horns,
That scrunch and scrape, and goggle and gape,
Are up my sleeve, I firmly believe—
And I'm horribly rimy and grimy.

III.

I'm sick of the strand, and the sand, and the band,
And the niggers and jiggers and dodgers ;
And the cigars of rather doubtful brand ;
And my landlady's "rights,"
And the frequent fights
On wretched points
Of ends of joints,
Which disappear, with my brandy and beer,
In a way that, to say the least, is queer.
And to mingle among the throng I long,
And to poke my joke and warble my song—
But there's no one near
On sands or pier,
For everyone's gone and I'm left alone,
The Last of the Seaside Lodgers !

NOTE BY OUR MAN OUT OF TOWN.—Watering places—resorts where the visitor is pumped dry.

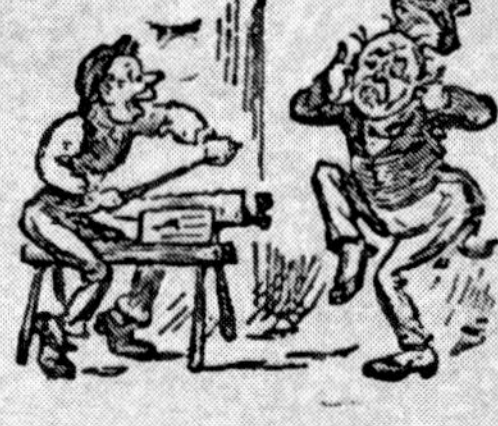

FILEY

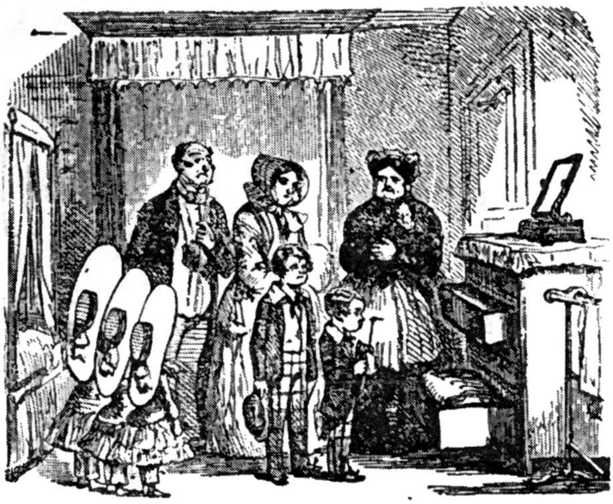

CROWDED STATE OF LODGING HOUSES

Lodging-House Keeper. "On'y this room to let, mem. A four-post—a tent,—and a very comfortable double-bedded chest of drawers for the young gentlemen."

A WET DAY AT THE SEASIDE

WHY does not some benefactor to his species discover and publish to a grateful world some rational way of spending a wet day at the sea-side? Why should it be something so unutterably miserable and depressing that its mere recollection afterwards makes one shudder?

This is the first really wet day that we have had

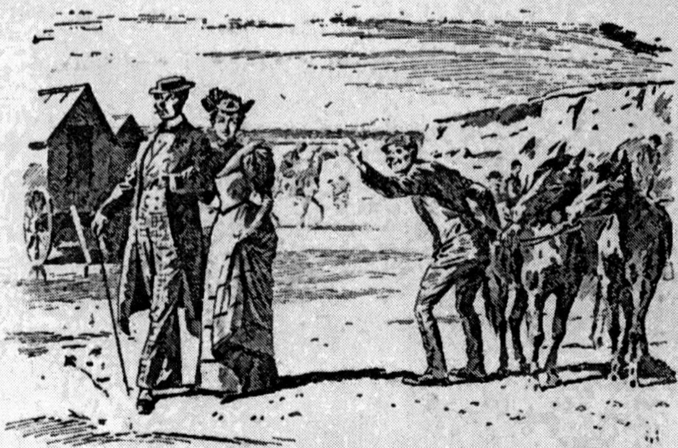

ON HIS HONEYMOON TOO!

Man with Sand Ponies. "Now then, Mister, you an' the young lady, a pony apiece? 'Ere y'are!"

Snobley (*loftily*). "Aw—I'm not accustomed to that class of animal."

Man (*readily*). "Ain't yer, sir? Ne' mind." (*To boy.*) "'Ere, Bill, look sharp! Gent 'll have a donkey!"

for a fortnight, but what a day! From morn to dewy eve, a summer's day, and far into the black night, the pitiless rain has poured and poured and poured. I broke the unendurable monotony of gazing from the weeping windows of my seaside lodging, by rushing out wildly and plunging madly into the rainy sea, and got drenched to the skin both going and returning. After changing everything, as people say but don't mean, and thinking

I saw something like a break in the dull leaden clouds, I again rushed out, and called on Jones, who has rooms in an adjacent terrace, and, with some difficulty, persuaded him to accompany me to the only billiard table in the miserable place. We both got gloriously wet on our way to this

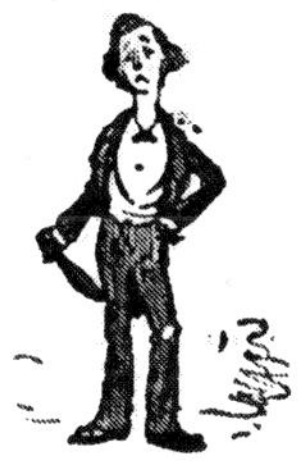

LOW-TIED

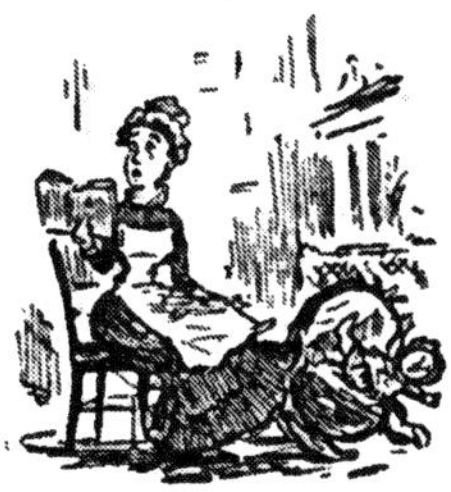

ROCKS

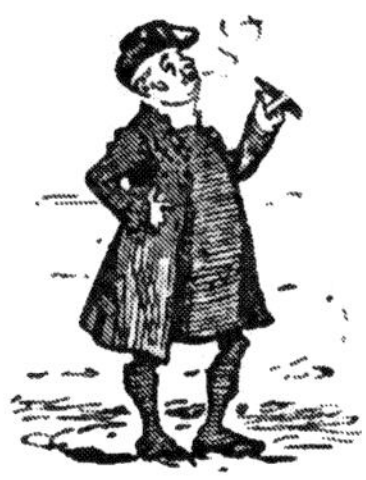

SEE-WEED

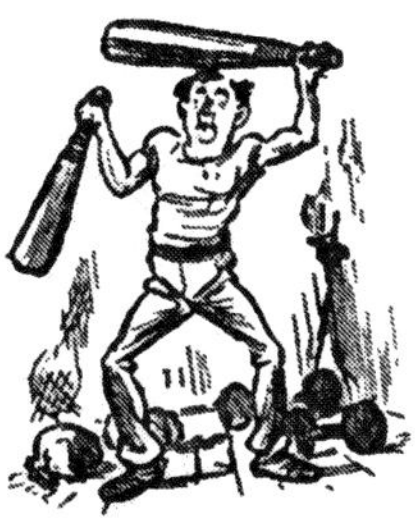

MUSCLE GATHERERS

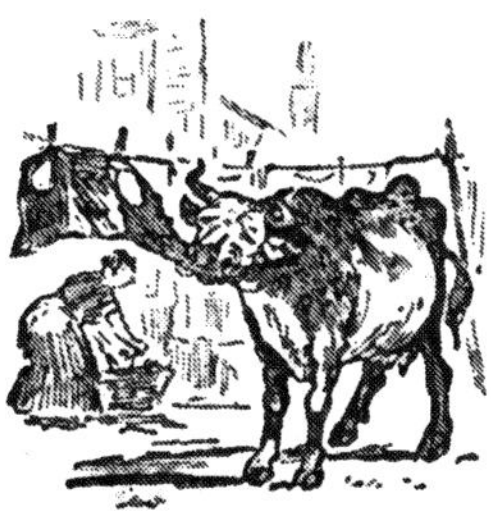

A KNAW WESTER

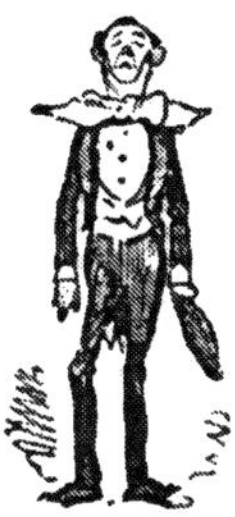

HIGH TIED

SEASIDE SPLITTERS

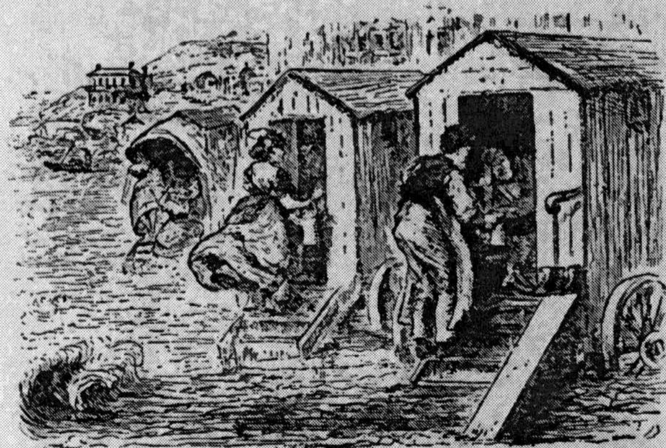

LIFE WOULD BE PLEASANT, BUT FOR ITS "PLEASURES."—*Sir Cornewall Lewis*

In consequence of the English watering-places being crowded, people are glad to find sleeping accommodation in the bathing-machines.

Boots (*from Jones's Hotel*). "I've brought your shaving water, sir; and you'll please to take care of your boots on the steps, gents: the tide's just a comin' in!"

haven of amusement, and were received with the pleasing intelligence that it was engaged by a private party of two, who had taken it until the rain ceased, and, when that most improbable event happened, two other despairing lodgers had secured the reversion. Another rush home, another drenching, another change of everything, except the weather, brought the welcome sight of dinner, over which we fondly lingered for nearly two mortal hours.

But one cannot eat all day long, even at the seaside on a wet day, and accordingly at four o'clock I was again cast upon my own resources.

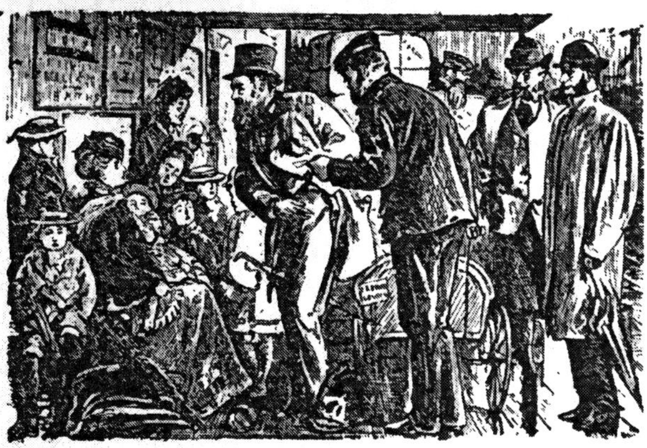

RETURNING HOME FROM THE SEASIDE

All the family have colds, except the under-nurse, who has a face-ache. Poor materfamilias, who originated the trip, is in despair at all the money spent for nothing, and gives way to tears. Paterfamilias endeavours to console her with the reflection that "*he* knew how it would be, but that, after all, St. John's Wood, where they live, is such a healthy place that, with care and doctoring, they *will soon be nearly as well as if they had never left it!*" [*Two gay bachelors may be seen contemplating paterfamilias and his little group. Their interest is totally untinged with envy.*]

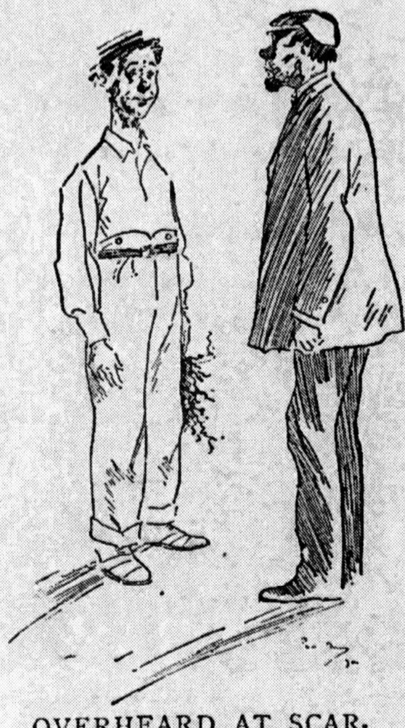

OVERHEARD AT SCARBOROUGH

"Do you know anything good for a cold?"

"Yes."

"What is it?"

"Have you got the price of two Scotch whiskies on you?"

"No."

"Then it's no use my telling you."

I received, I confess, a certain amount of grim satisfaction at seeing Brown—Bumptious Brown, as we call him in the City, he being a common councilman, or a liveryman, or something of that kind—pass by in a fly, with heaps of luggage and children, all looking so depressingly wet,—and if he had not the meanness to bring with him, in a half-dozen hamper,

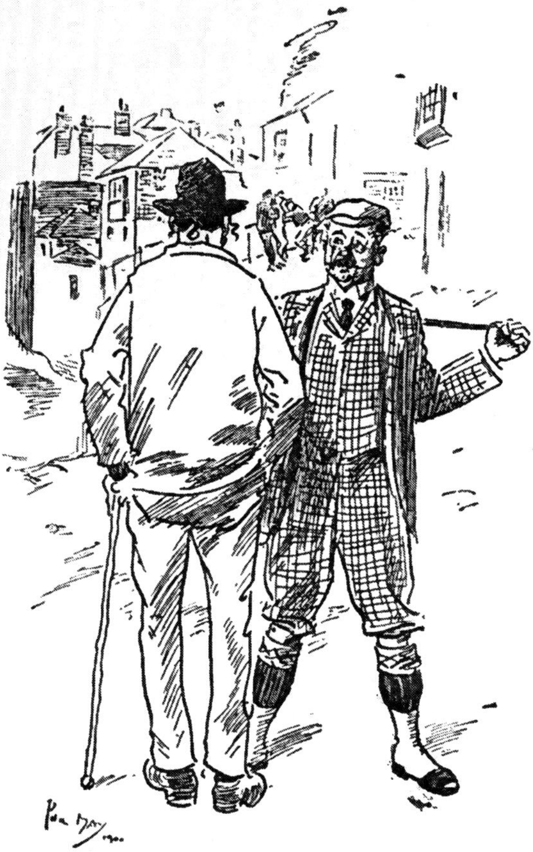

Snobson (*to inhabitant of out-of-way seaside resort*). "What sort of people do you get down here in the summer?"
Inhabitant. "Oh, all sorts, zur. There be fine people an' common people, an' some just half-an'-half, like yourself, zur."

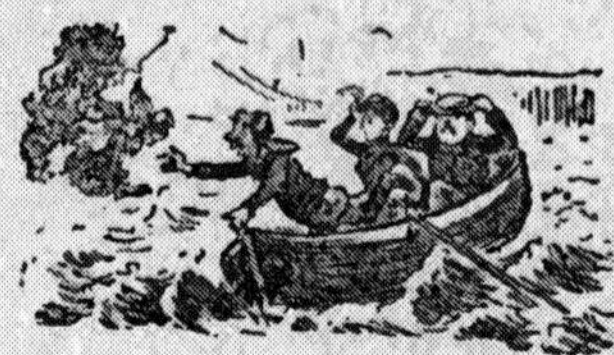

BOATMAN SECURING A LIVELY-HOOD

six bottles of his abominable Gladstone claret! He grinned at me as he passed, like a Chester cat, I think they call that remarkable animal, and I afterwards learnt the reason. He had been speculating for a rise in wheat, and, as he vulgarly said, the rain suited his book, and he only hoped it would last for a week or two! Ah! the selfishness of some men! What cared he about my getting wet through twice in one day, so long as it raised the price of his wretched wheat?

My wife coolly recommended me to read the second volume of a new novel she had got from the Library, called, I think, *East Glynne*, or some such name, but how can a man read in a room with four stout healthy boys and a baby, especially when the said baby is evidently very uncomfortable, and the four boys are playing at leap-frog? Women have this wonderful faculty, my wife to a remarkable extent. I have often, with unfeigned astonishment, seen her apparently lost in the sentimental troubles

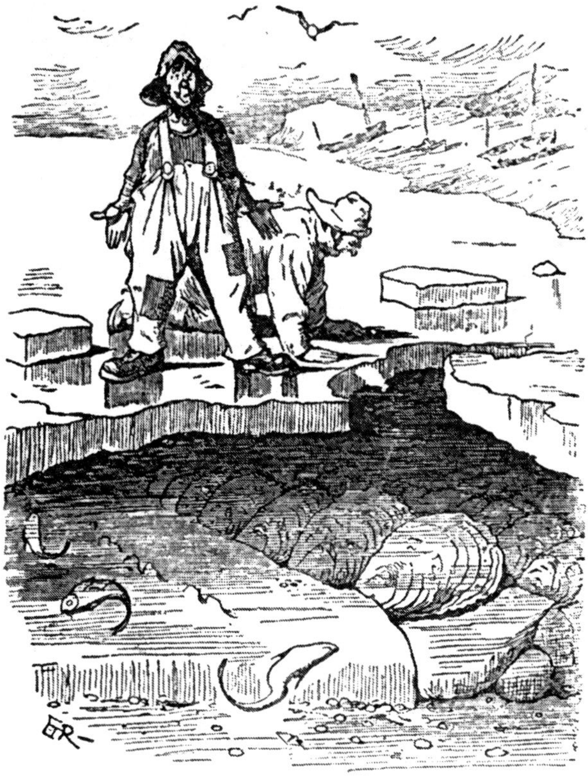

THE OYSTERS AT WHITSTABLE FROZEN IN THEIR BEDS!

(*See Daily Papers*)

of some imaginary heroine, while the noisy domestic realities around her have gone on unheeded.

I again took my place at the window, and gazed upon the melancholy sea, and remembered, with a smile of bitter irony, how I had agreed to pay an extra guinea a week for the privilege of facing the sea!—and such a sea! It was, of course, very low water—it generally is at this charming place; and the sea had retired to its extremest distance, as if utterly ashamed of its dull, damp, melancholy

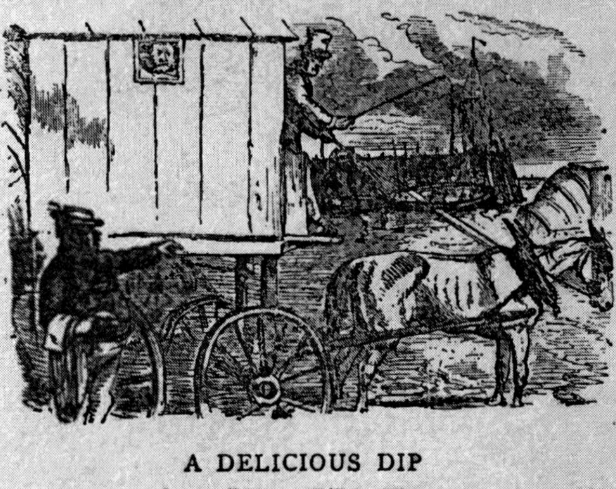

A DELICIOUS DIP

Bathing Attendant. "Here, Bill! The gent wants to be took out deep—take 'im *into the drain!!*"

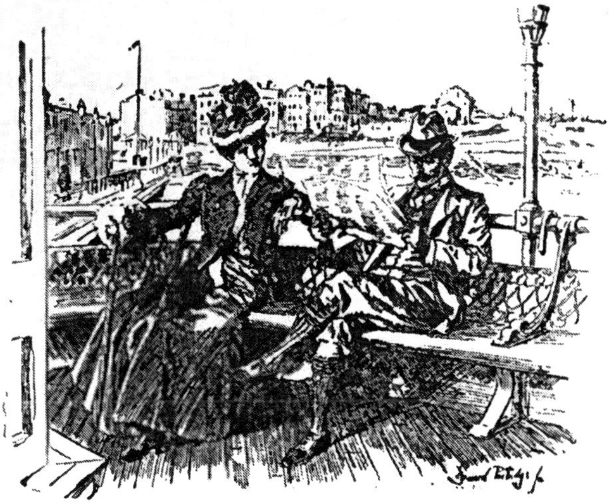

She. "How much was old Mr. Baskerville's estate sworn at by his next-of-kin?"
He. "Oh—a pretty good lot."
She. "Really? Why, I heard he died worth hardly anything!"
He. "Yes, so he did—that's just it."

appearance. And there stood that ridiculous apology for a pier, with its long, lanky, bandy legs, on which I have been dragged every evening to hear the band play. Such a band! The poor wheezy cornet was bad enough, but the trombone, with its two notes that it jerked out like the snorts of a starting train, was a caution. Oh! that poor "*Sweetheart,*" with which we were favoured every evening! I always pictured her to myself sitting at a window listening, enraptured, to a serenade from that trombone!

But there's no band to-night, not a solitary promenader on the bandy-legged pier, I even doubt if the pier master is sitting as usual at the receipt of custom, and I pull down the blind, to shut out the miserable prospect, with such an energetic jerk that I bring down the whole complicated

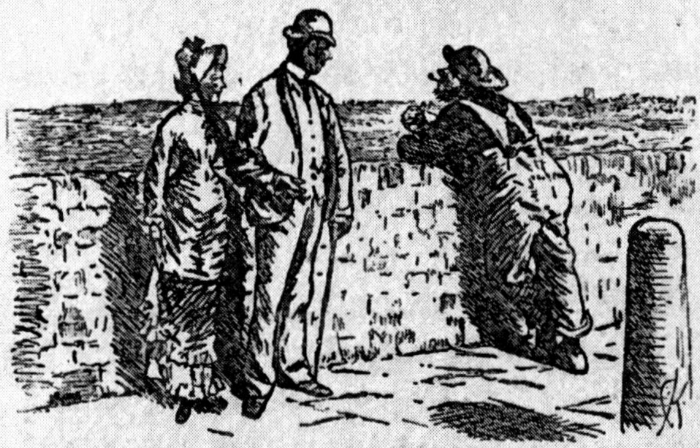

EVIDENCE OLFACTORY

Angelina (*scientific*). "Do you smell the iodine from the sea, Edwin? Isn't it refreshing?"

Old Salt (*overhearing*). "What you smell ain't the sea, miss. It's the town drains as flows out just 'ere!"

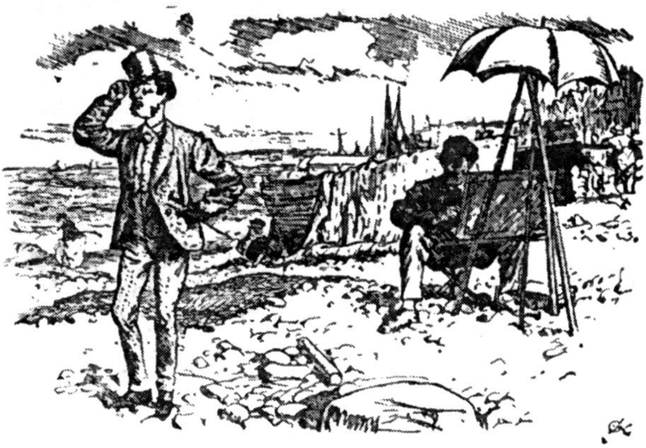

OBLIGING

Excursionist (to himself). "Ullo! 'ere's one o' them artists. 'Dessay 'e'll want a genteel figger for 'is foreground. I'll *stand for 'im !!!*"

machinery, and nearly frighten baby into a fit, while the four irreverent boys indulge in a loud guffaw.

Thank goodness, on Saturday I exchange our miserable, wheezy, asthmatic band for the grand orchestra of the Covent Garden Promenade Concerts, and the awful perfume of rotten seaweed for the bracing atmosphere of glorious London.

AN OUTSIDER.

TRUE DIPSOMANIA.—Overbathing at the seaside.

AN IDLE HOLIDAY

WHEN the days are bright and hot,
In the month of August,
When the sunny hours are not
Marred by any raw gust,
Then I turn from toil with glee,
Sing a careless canto,
And to somewhere by the sea
Carry my portmanteau.

Shall I, dreaming on the sand,
Pleased with all things finite,
Envy Jones who travels and
Climbs an Apennine height—
Climbs a rugged peak with pain,
Literally speaking,
Only to descend again
Fagged with pleasure-seeking?

Smith, who, worn with labour, went
Off for rest and leisure,
Races round the Continent
In pursuit of pleasure:
Having lunched at Bâle, he will
At Lucerne his tea take,
Riding till he's faint and ill,
Tramping till his feet ache.

Shall I, dreaming thus at home,
Left ashore behind here,
Envy restless men who roam
Seeking what I find here?

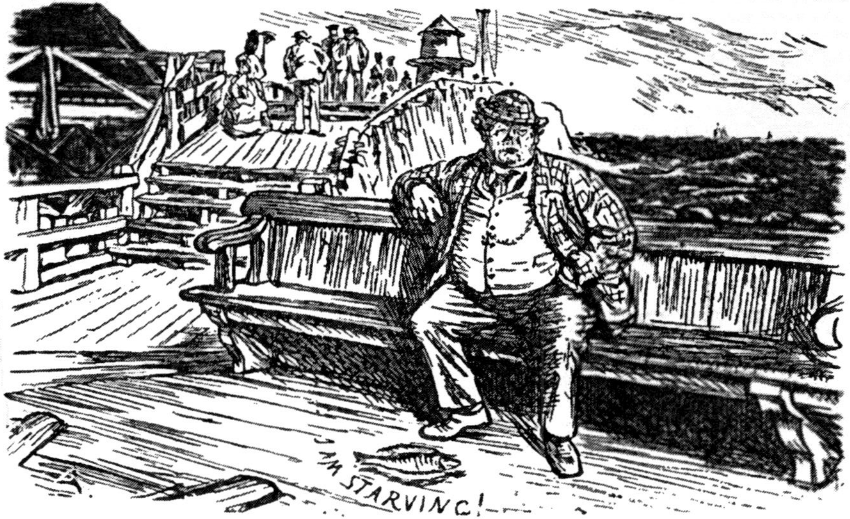

SUSPICION

Stout Visitor (on discovering that, during his usual nap after luncheon, he has been subjected to a grossly personal practical joke). "It's one o' those dashed artists that are staying at the 'Lord Nelson' 'a' done this, I know!"

Since beside my native sea,
Where I sit to woo it,
Pleasure always comes to me,
Why should I pursue it?

THE MURMUR OF THE TIED

EXTRA SPECIAL.—*Paterfamilias* (*inspecting bill, to landlady*). I thought you said, Mrs. Buggins, when I took these apartments, that there were no extras, but here I find boots, lights, cruets, fire, table-linen, sheets, blankets and kitchen fire charged.

Mrs. Buggins. Lor' bless you, sir, they're not extras, but necessaries.

Paterfamilias. What, then, do you consider extras?

Mrs. Buggins. Well, sir, that's a difficult question to answer, but I should suggest salad oil, fly-papers, and turtle soup.

[*Paterfamilias drops the subject and pays his account.*

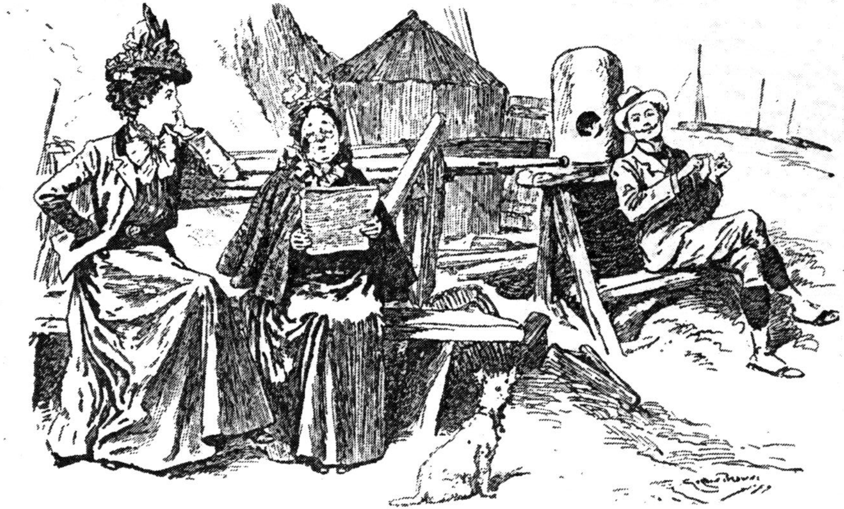

Aunt Jane. "It's wonderful how this wireless telegraphy is coming into use!"

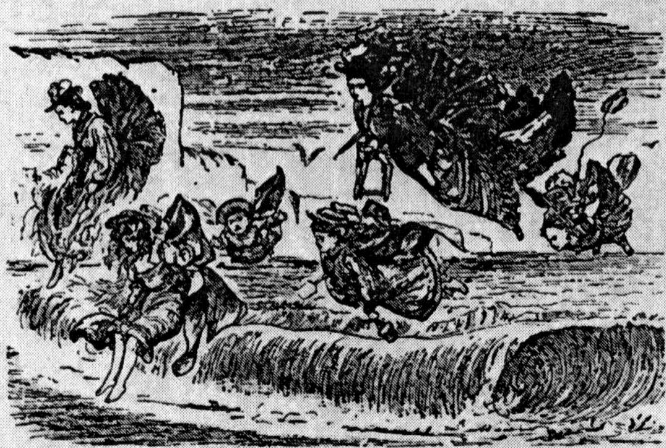

A DREAM OF THE SEA

Ethel, who is not to have a seaside trip this year, dreams every night that she and her mamma and aunt and sisters spread their sash-bows and panniers and fly away to the yellow sands.

THE MARGATE BATHING-WOMAN'S LAMENT

It nearly broke my widowed art,
  When first I tuk the notion,
That parties didn't as they used,
  Take reglar to the ocean.

The hinfants, darling little soles,
  Still cum quite frequent, bless 'em!
But they is only sixpence each,
  Which hardly pays to dress 'em.

The reason struck me all at once,
  Says I, "It's my opinion,
The grown-up folks no longer bathes
  Because of them vile Sheenions."

The last as cum drest in that style,
  Says, as she tuk it horf her,
" I'm sure I shall not know the way
  To re-arrange my quoffur ! "

By which she ment the ed of air,
  Which call it wot they will, sir ;
Cum doubtless off a convict at
  Millbank or Pentonville, sir.

The Parliament should pass a law,
  Which there's sufficient reason ;
That folks as wear the Sheenions should
  Bathe reg'lar in the season.

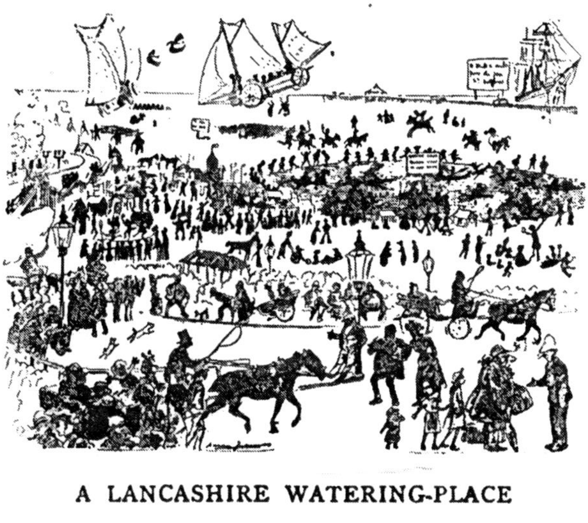

A LANCASHIRE WATERING-PLACE

"MERRY MARGIT"

(*Another communication from the side of the dear sea waves*)

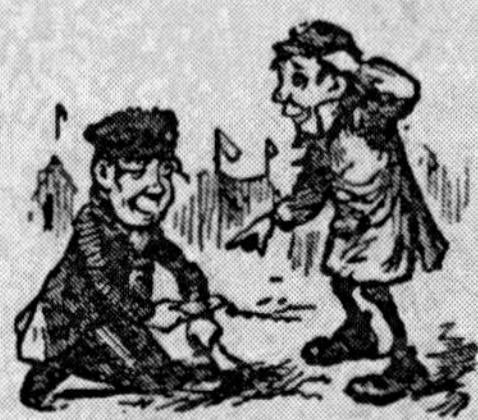

DEAL

I WAS told it was greatly improved—that there were alterations in the sea-front suggestive of the best moments of the Thames Embankment—that quite "smart" people daily paraded the pier. So having had enough of "Urn-bye," I moved on. The improvements scarcely made themselves felt at the railway station. Seemingly they had not attracted what Mr. Jeames would call "the upper suckles." There were the customary British middle-class matron from Peckham, looking her sixty summers to the full in a sailor hat; the seaside warrior first cousin to the billiard-marker captain with flashy rings, beefy hands, and a stick of pantomime proportions, and the theatrical lady whose connection with the stage I imagine was confined to

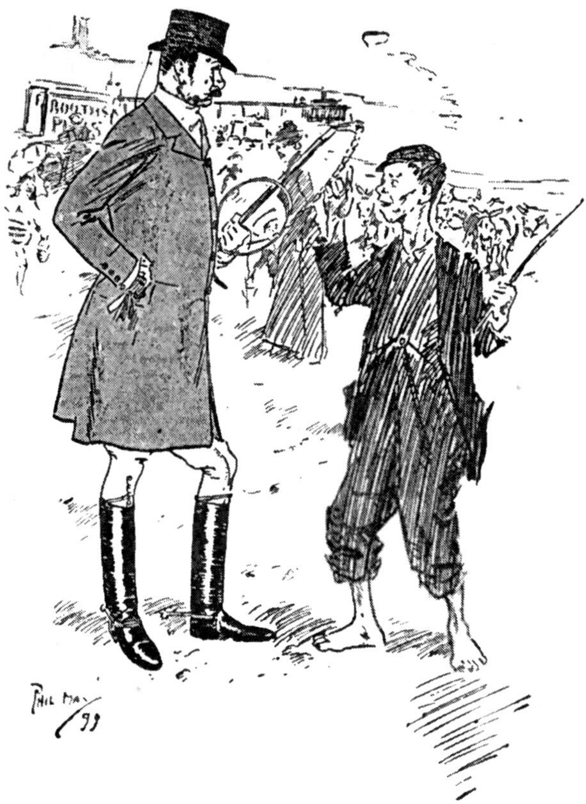

Boy (*to Brown, who is exceedingly proud of his sporting appearance*). "Want a donkey, mister?"

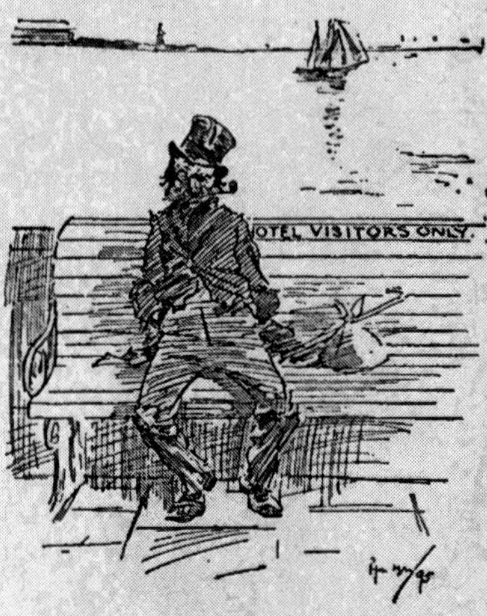

"NICE FOR THE VISITORS"
(Sketch outside a fashionable hotel)

capering before the footlights. However, they all were there, as I had seen them any summer these twenty years.

But I had been told to go to the Pier, and so to the Pier I went, glancing on my way at the entertainers on the sands, many of whom I found to be old friends. Amongst them was the "h"-less phrenologist, whose insight into character apparently satisfied the parents of any child whose head he selected to examine. Thus, if he said that a particularly stupid-looking little boy would make a good architect, schoolmaster, or traveller for fancy goods, a gentleman in an alpaca-coat and a wide-awake hat would bow gratified acquiescence, a demonstration that would also be evoked from a lady in a dust cloak, when the lecturer insisted that a giggling little girl would make a "first-rate dressmaker and cutter-out."

Arrived at the Pier, I found there was twopence to pay for the privilege of using the extension, which included a restaurant, a band, some talented

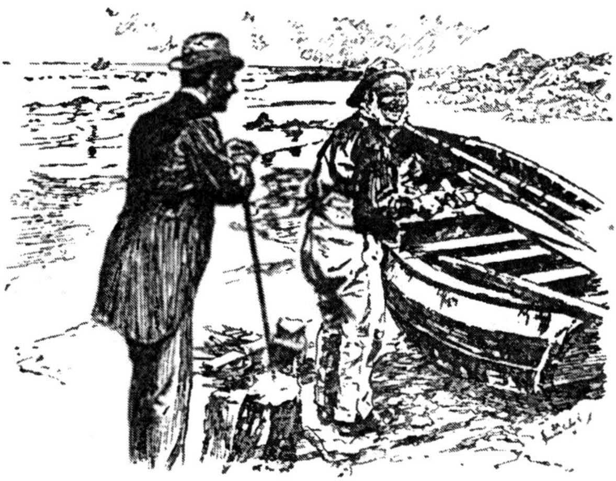

INCORRIGIBLE

Visitor. "Well, my man, I expect it must have cost you a lot of money to paint your nose that colour!"

Reprobate. "Ah, an' if Oi cud affoord it, Oi'd have it *varnished* now!"

fleas, and a shop with a window partly devoted to the display of glass tumblers, engraved with legends of an amusing character, such as "Good old Mother-in-Law," "Jack's Night Cap," "Aunt Julia's Half Pint," and so on. There were a number of seats and shelters, and below the level of the shops was a landing-stage, at which twice a day two steamers from or to London removed or landed passengers.

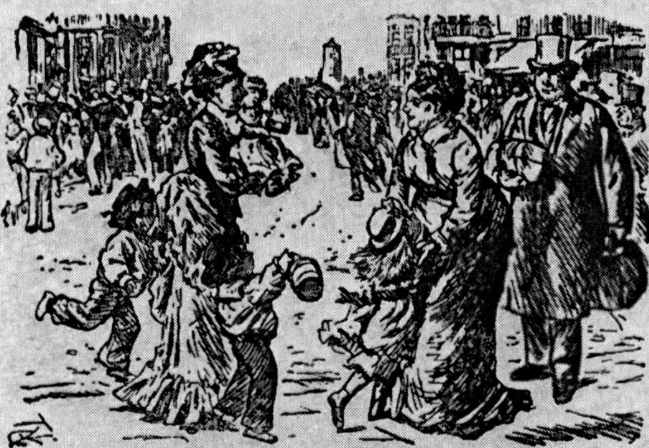

"NO ACCOUNTING FOR TASTE"

Materfamilias (*just arrived at Shrimpville—the children had been down a month before*). "Well, Jane, have you found it dull?"

Nurse. "It was at fust, M'm. There was nothink to improve the mind, M'm, till the niggers come down!!"

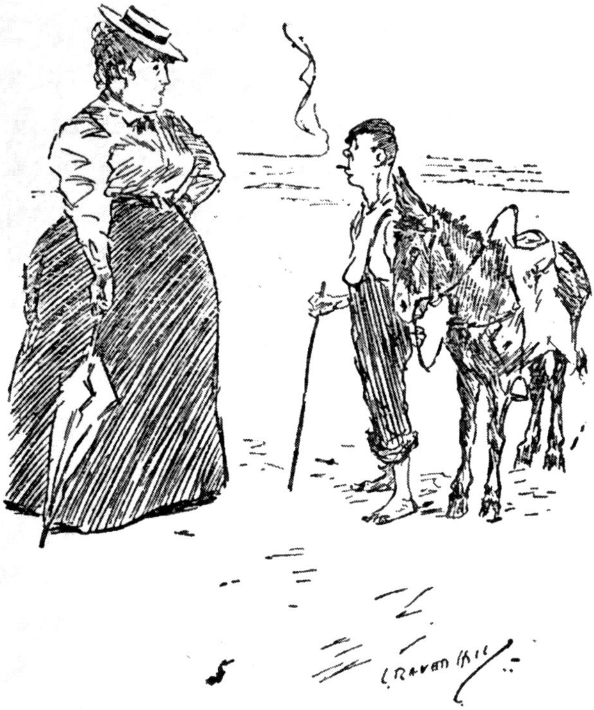

BY THE SAD SEA WAVES

"But, are you sure?"
"Yus, lady. 'E 's strong as an 'orse!"
"But how am I to get on?"
"Oh, *I'll lift yer!*"

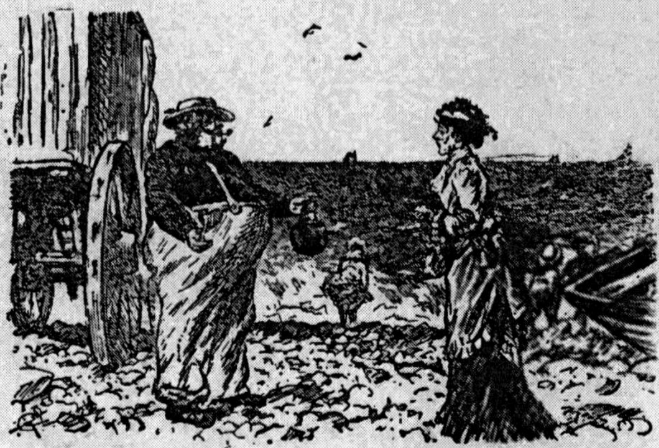

DELICATE ATTENTION

Confiding Spinster. "I'm afraid the sea is too cold for me this morning, Mr. Swabber."

Bathing Man. "Cold, miss! Lor' bless yer, I just took and powered a kittle o' bilin' water in to take the chill off when I see you a comin'!"

During the rest of the four-and-twenty hours it seemed to be occupied by a solitary angler, catching chiefly seaweed. The Band, in spite of its uniform, was not nearly so military as that at "Urn Bye." It contained a pianoforte—an instrument upon which I found the young gentleman who sold the programmes practising during a pause between the morning's selection and the afternoon's performances. But still the Band was a very tuneful one, and increased the pleasure that the presence of so many delightful promenaders was bound to produce. Many of the ladies who walked round and round, talking courteously to 'Arry in all his varieties, wore men's *habits, pur et simple* (giving them the semblance of appearing in their shirt-sleeves), while their heads were adorned with fair wigs and sailor hats, apparently fixed on together.

These free-and-easy-looking damsels did not

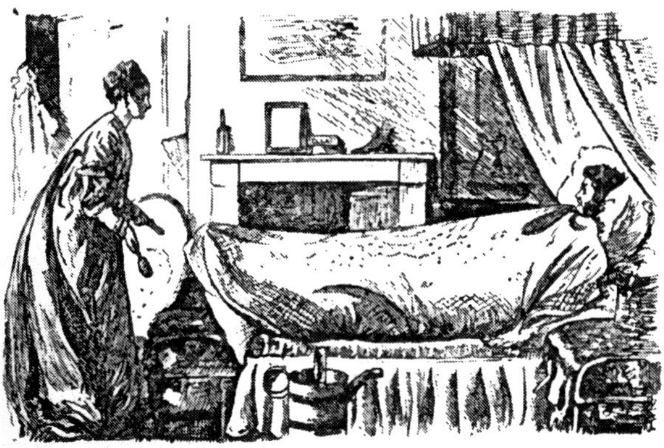

HOLIDAY PLEASURES

Injured Individual. "Heigho! I *did* think I should find some refuge from the miseries of the seaside in the comforts of a bed! Just look where my feet are, Maria!"

His Wife. "*Well*, John! it's *only* for a *month*, you know!"

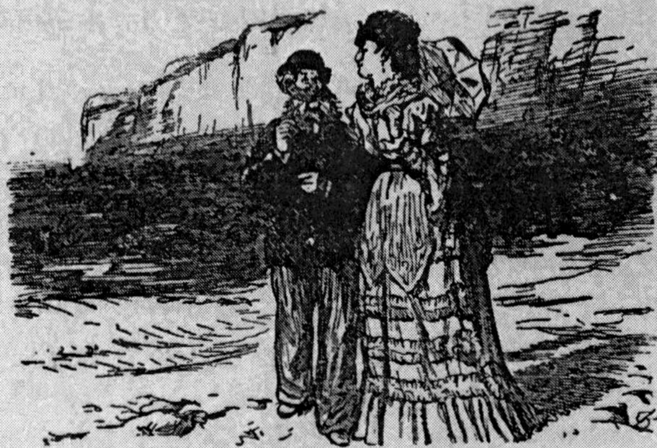

BLIGHTED HOPES

Extract of letter from Laura to Lillie:—"I declare, dear, I never gave the absurd creature the slightest encouragement. I did say, one evening, I thought the little sandy coves about Wobbleswick were charming, especially one. *The idea!*—of his thinking I was alluding to him!"——&c., &c.

seem to find favour in the eyes of certain other ladies of a sedater type, who regarded them (over their novels) with undisguised contempt. These other ladies, I should think, from their conversation and appearance, must have been the very flowers of the flock of Brixton Rise, and the *crême de la crême* of Peckham Rye society. Of course there were a number of more or less known actors and actresses from London, some of them enjoying

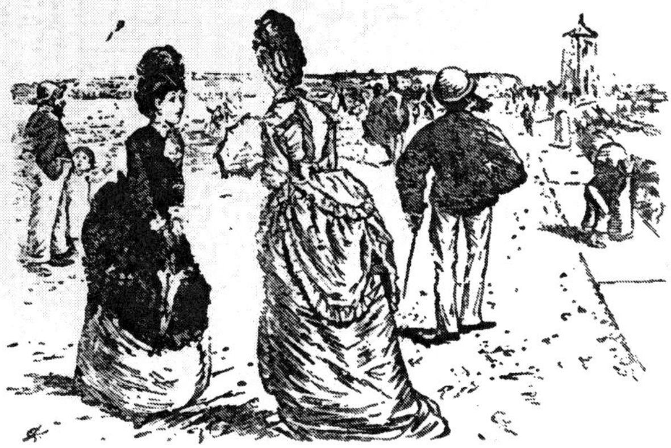

SENSITIVE

"I think I told you, in my letter of the first of October, of his absurd interpretation of an innocent remark of mine about the sandy shores of Wobbleswick. Well, would you believe it, dear! we were strolling on the Esplanade, the other day, when he suddenly left Kate and me, and took himself off in a tremendous huff because we said we liked walking *with an object!!*"

[*Extract from a later letter of Laura's to Lillie.*

a brief holiday, and others engaged in the less lucrative occupation of "resting."

However, the dropping of "h's," even to the accompaniment of sweet music, sooner or later becomes monotonous, and so, after awhile, I was glad to leave the Pier for the attractions of the Upper Cliff. On my way I passed a Palace of Pleasure or Varieties, or Something wherein a twopenny wax-work show seemed at the moment to be one of its greatest attractions. This show contained a Chamber of Horrors, a scene full of quiet humour of Napoleon the Third Lying in State, and an old effigy of George the Third. The collection included the waxen head of a Nonconformist minister, who, according to the lecturer, had been "wery good to the poor," preserved in a small deal-box. There was also the "Key-Dyevie" of Egypt, General Gordon, and Mrs. Maybrick. Tearing myself away from these miscellaneous memories of the past, I ascended to the East Cliff, which had still the

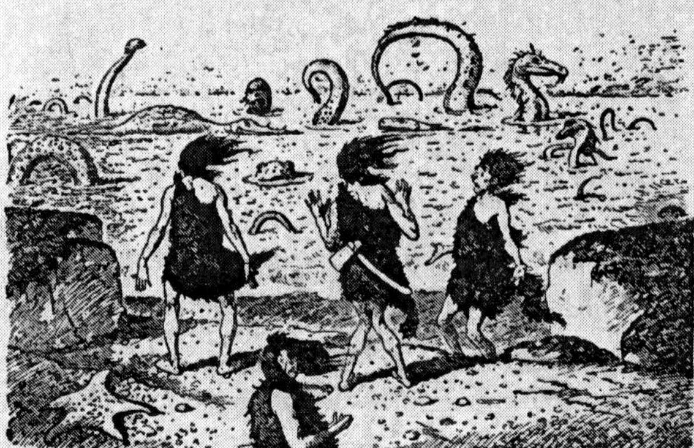

PREHISTORIC PEEPS

"No bathing to-day!"

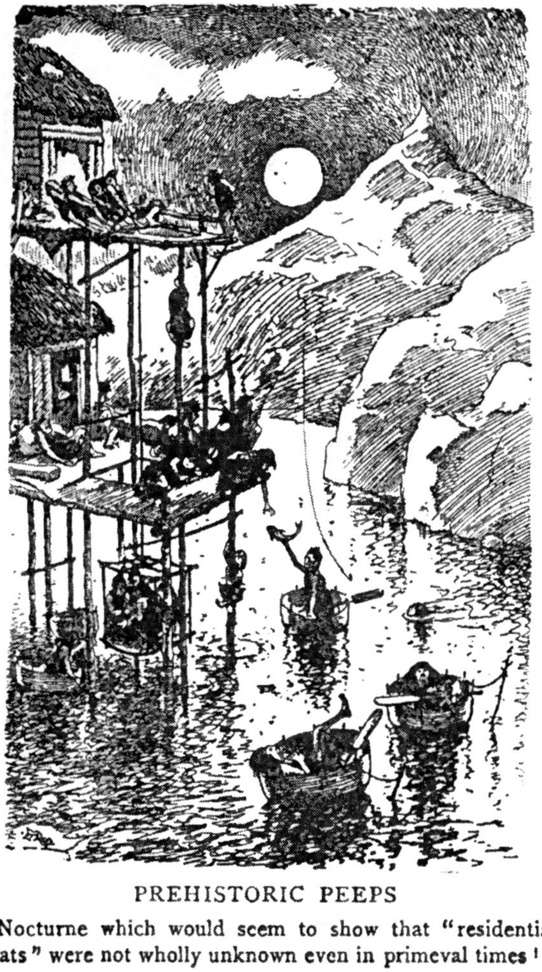

PREHISTORIC PEEPS

A Nocturne which would seem to show that "residential flats" were not wholly unknown even in primeval times!

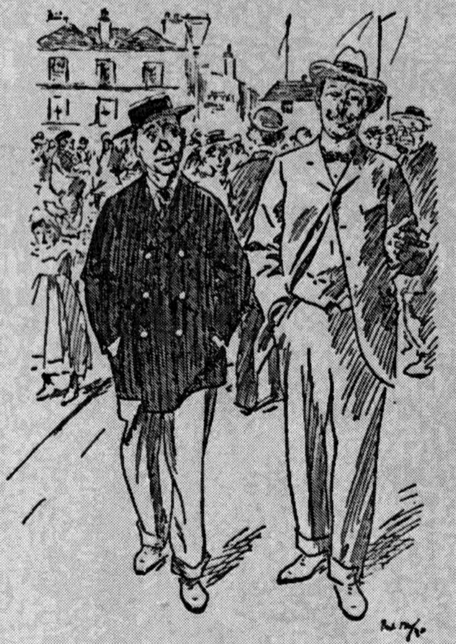

Blinks. "The sun 'll be over the yard-arm in ten minutes. *Then* we'll have a drink!"

Jinks. "I think I'll have one while I'm waiting!"

"apartments-furnished" look that was wont to distinguish it of yore. There was no change there; and as I walked through the town, which once, as a watering-place, was second only in importance to Bath,—which a century ago had for its M.C. a rival of Beau Nash,—I could not help thinking how astonished the ghosts of the fine ladies and gentlemen who visited "Meregate" in 1789 must be, if they are able to see their successors of to-day—"Good Old Chawlie Cadd," and Miss Topsie Stuart Plantagenet, *née* Tompkins.

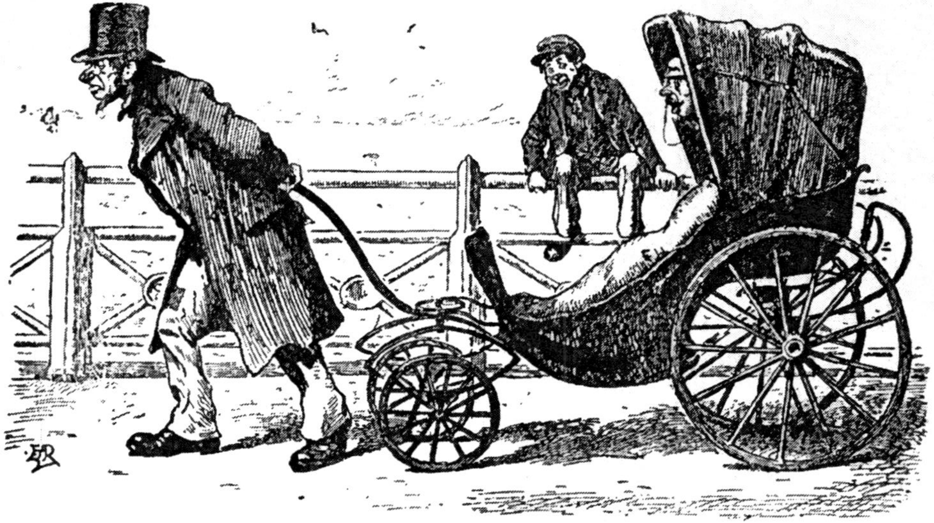

TRIALS OF A CONVALESCENT

Tompkins (*in a feeble voice, for the fourth or fifth time, with no result*). "Chairman!!! chairman!!!"

That Awful Boy. "Lydies and gentlemen——!!"

SEASIDE ASIDES

(Paterfamilias in North Cornwall)

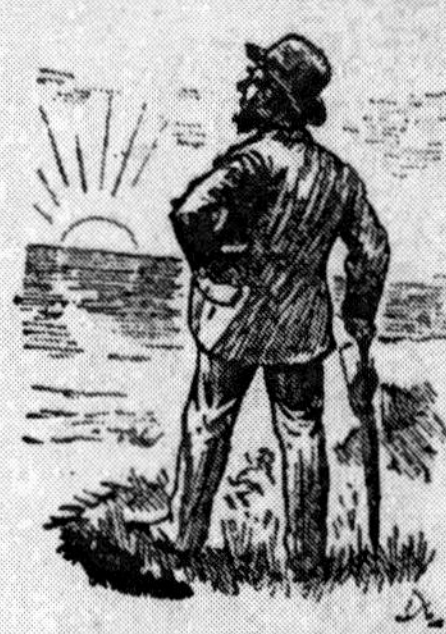

OH! how delightful now at last to come
Away from town—its dirt, its degradation,
Its never-ending whirl, its ceaseless hum.
(A long chalks better, though, than sheer stagnation.)

For what could mortal man or maid want more
Than breezy downs to stroll on, rocks to climb up,
Weird labyrinthine caverns to explore?
(There's nothing else to do to fill the time up.)

Your honest face here earns an honest brown,
You ramble on for miles 'mid gorse and heather,
Sheep hold athletic sports upon the down
(Which makes the mutton taste as tough as leather).

The place is guiltless, too, of horrid piers.
And likewise is not Christy-Minstrel tooney;
No soul-distressing strains disturb your ears.
(A German band has just played "*Annie Rooney.*")

The eggs as fresh as paint, the Cornish cream
The boys from school all say is "simply ripping."
The butter, so the girls declare, "a dream."
(The only baccy you can buy quite dripping.)

A happiness of resting after strife,
Where one forgets all worldly pain and sorrow,
And one contentedly could pass one's life.
(A telegram will take *me* home to-morrow.)

SCENE : MARGATE BEACH ON EASTER MONDAY. —*First Lady.* "Oh, here comes a steamer. How high she is out of the water."

Second Lady. "Yes, dear, but don't you see? It's because the tide's so low."

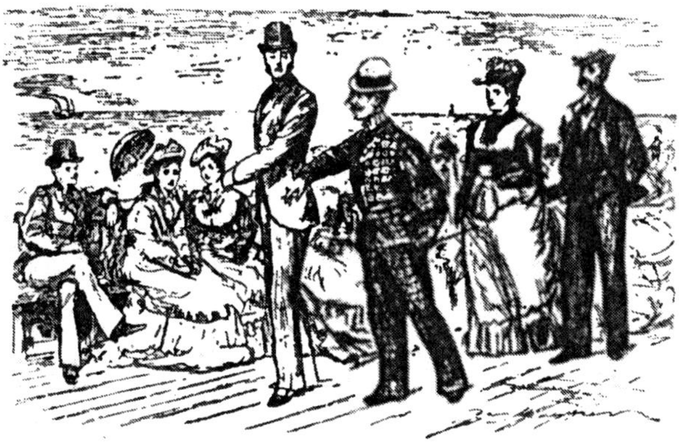

AWKWARD

The aristocratic Jones (*rather ashamed of his loud acquaintance, Brown*). "You must excuse me, but if there's one thing in the world I particularly object to, it's to having anybody take my arm!"

Brown. "All right, old fellow!—*you* take *mine!*"

THE SEASIDE VISITOR'S VADE MECUM

Question. Is it your intention to leave London at once to benefit by the ocean breezes on the English coast?

Answer. Certainly, with the bulk of my neighbours.

Q. Then the metropolis will become empty?

A. Practically, for only about three and a half

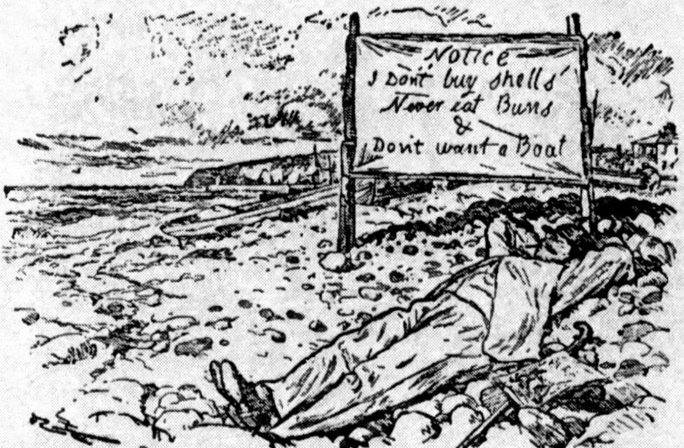

PARIS?

"Not if I know it! Give me a quiet month at the seaside, and leave me alone, please!"

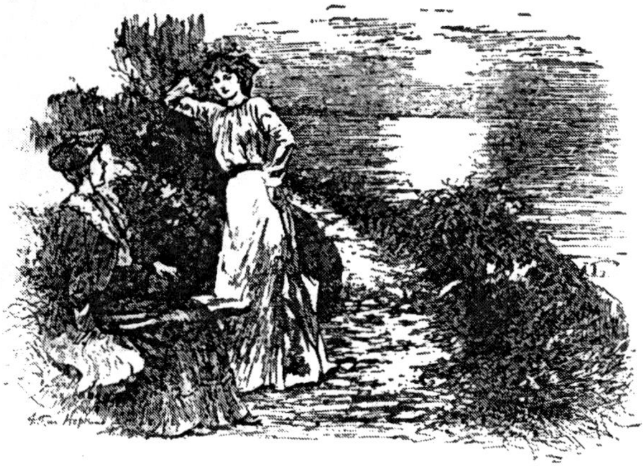

CONVERSATIONAL PITFALLS

Irene. "Do you remember Kitty Fowler?"
Her Friend. "No, I don't."
Irene. "Oh, you *must* remember Kitty. She was the plainest girl in Torquay. But I forgot—that was after you left!"

millions out of the four millions will be left behind.

Q. What do you consider the remaining residuum?

A. From a West End point of view a negligible quantity.

Q. Do not some of the Eastenders visit the seaside?

A. Yes, at an earlier period in the year, when

they pay rather more for their accommodation than their neighbours of the West.

Q. How can this be, if it be assumed that the East is poorer than the West?

A. The length of the visit is governed by the

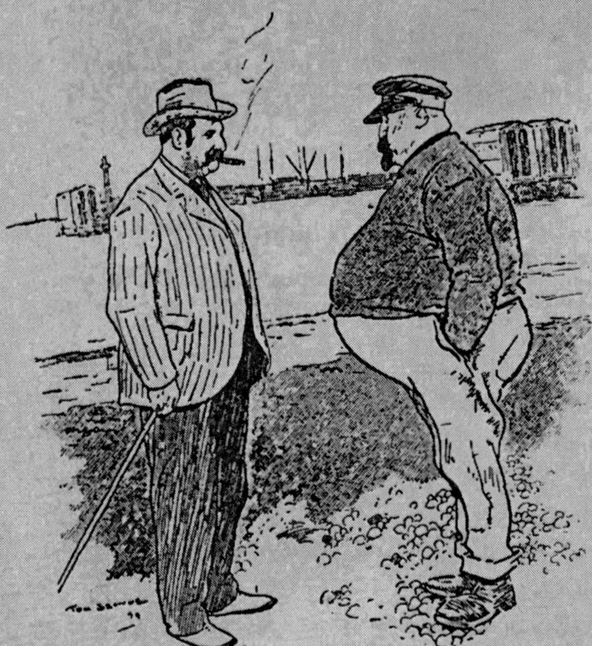

Visitor. "Have you ever seen the sea-serpent?"
Boatman. "No, sir. I'm a temperance man."

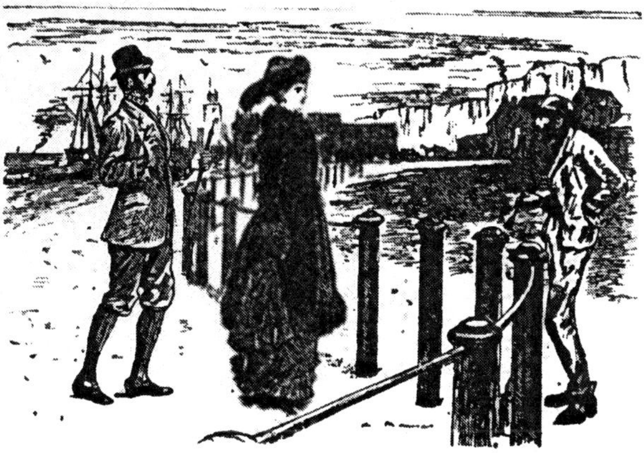

SEPARATE INTERESTS

Husband. "Hi! Maria! Take care of the paint!"
Painter. "It don't matter, ma'am. It'll all 'ave to be painted again!"

weight of the purse. Belgravia stays a couple of months at Eastbourne, while three days at Margate is enough for Shoreditch.

Q. Has a sojourn by the sea waves any disadvantages?

A. Several. In the first instance, lodgings are frequently expensive and uncomfortable. Then there is always a chance that the last lodgers may have occupied their rooms as convalescents. Lastly, it is not invariably the case that the climate

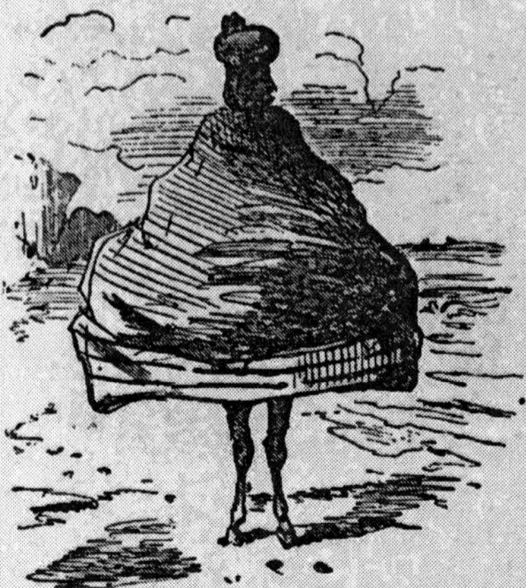

CAUTION TO YOUNG LADIES WHO RIDE IN CRINOLINE ON DONKEYS

agrees with himself and his family.

Q. And what becomes of the house in town?

A. If abandoned to a caretaker, the reception rooms may be used by her own family as best chambers, and if let to strangers, the furniture may be injured irretrievably.

Q. But surely in the last case there would be the certainty of pecuniary indemnity?

A. Cherished relics cannot be restored by their commonplace value in money.

Q. Then, taking one thing with another, the benefit of a visit to the seaside is questionable?

A. Assuredly; and an expression of heartfelt

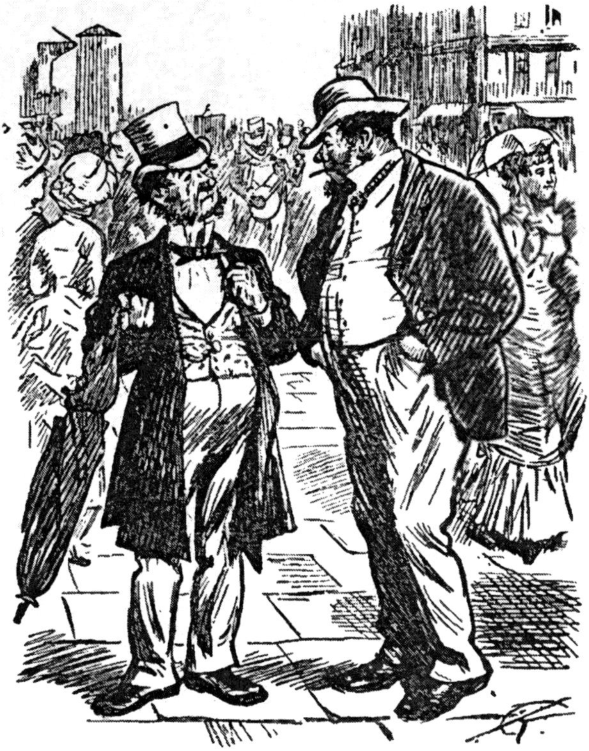

MARGATE

Chatty Visitor. "I like the place. I always come here. 'Worst of it is, it's a little too dressy!'

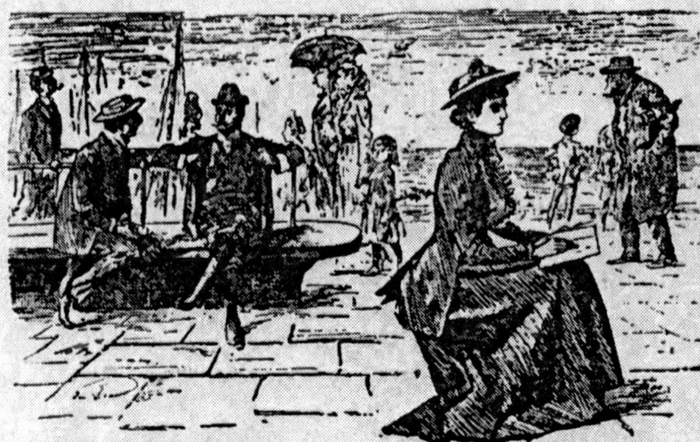

UNLUCKY COMPLIMENTS

Shy but Susceptible Youth. "Er—*could* you tell me who that young lady is—sketching?"

Affable Stranger. "She has the misfortune to be my wife!"

Shy but Susceptible One (*desperately anxious to please, and losing all presence of mind*). "Oh—the misfortune's entirely *yours*, I'm *sure!*"

delight at the termination of the outing and the consequent return home is the customary finish to the, styled by courtesy, holiday.

Q. But has not the seaside visit a compensating advantage?

A. The seaside visit has a compensating advantage of overwhelming proportions, which completely swallows up and effaces all suggestions of discomfort—it is the fashion.

BRILLIANT SUGGESTION (*Overheard at the Seaside*).—*She.* "So much nicer now that all the visitors have gone. Don't you think so?"

He. "Yes, by Jove! So jolly nice and quiet! Often wonder that *everybody* doesn't come now when there's nobody here, don't you know!"

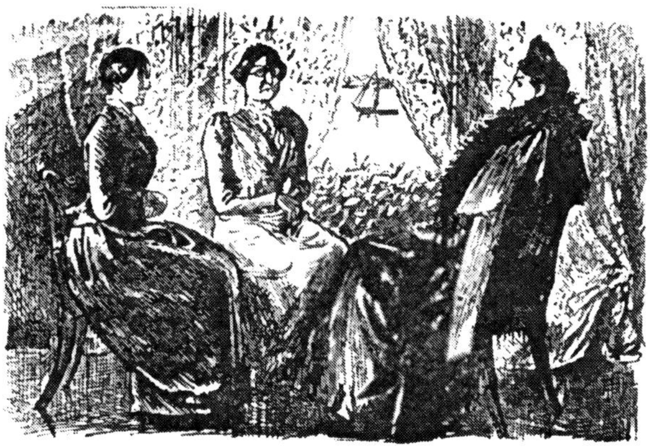

A NUISANCE

Miss Priscilla. "Yes; it's a beautiful view. But tourists are in the habit of bathing on the opposite shore, and that's rather a drawback."

Fair Visitor. "Dear me! but at such a distance as that—surely——"

Miss Priscilla. "Ah, but with a *telescope*, you know!"

THE SEASIDE PHOTOGRAPHER

I DO not mean the Kodak fiend,
  Who takes snap-shots of ladies dipping,
And gloats o'er sundry views he's gleaned
  Of amatory couples "tripping."

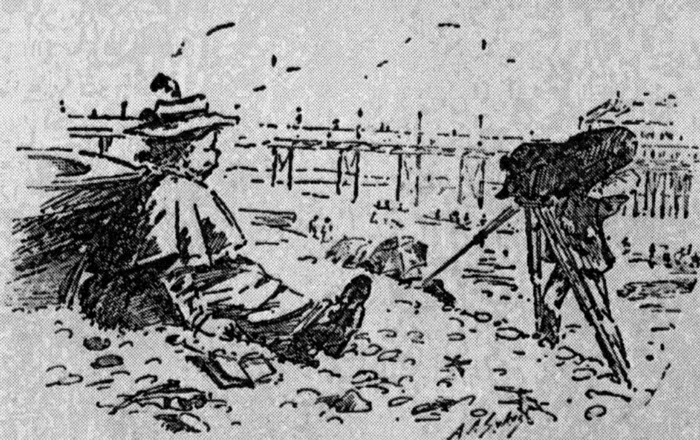

No, not these playful amateurs
  I sing of, but the serious artist,
Who spreads upon the beach his lures,
  What time the season 's at its smartest.

His tongue is glib, his terms are cheap,
  For ninepence while you wait he 'll take you ;
Posterity shall, marv'lling, keep
  The "tin-type" masterpiece he'll make you.

What though his camera be antique,
  His dark-room just a nose-bag humble,
What if his tripod legs are weak,
  And threaten constantly to tumble.

No swain nor maiden can withstand
His invitation arch, insidious,
To pose *al fresco* on the strand—
His *clientèle* are not fastidious.

"You are so lovely," says the wretch,
"Your picture will be quite entrancing!"
And to the lady in the sketch
I overheard him thus romancing.

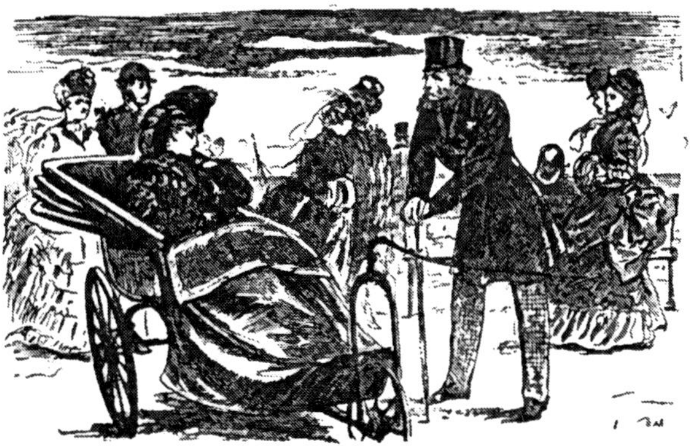

THE RULING PASSION

Sir Talbot Howard Vere de Vere. "Ah! Good morning, Mrs. Jones! Dreadful accident just occurred. Poor young lady riding along the King's Road--horse took fright—reared, and fell back upon her—dreadfully injured, I'm sorry to say!"

Mrs. Woodbee Swellington Jones. "*Quite* too shocking, dear Sir Talbot! Was she—er—a person of position?"

Sir Talbot Howard Vere de Vere. "POSITION, by George!! Dooced uncomfortable position, too, I should say!"

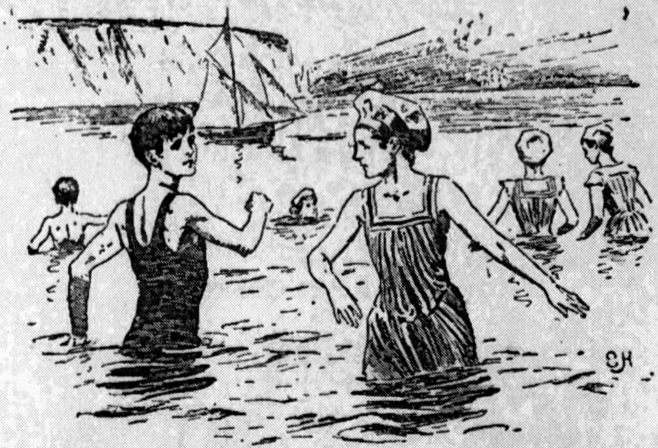

FOR THE PUBLIC GOOD

Bertie. "Gertie, do just go back to the beach and fetch me a baby (you'll find a lot about), and I'll show you all the different ways of saving it from drowning!"

ANNALS OF A WATERING-PLACE

THAT HAS "SEEN ITS DAY"

THE weather which, in Mr. Dunstable's varied experience of five-and-twenty years, he assures me, has never been so bad, having at length afforded some indications of "breaking," I make the acquaintance, through Mrs. Cobbler, of Mr. Wisterwhistle, proprietor of the one bath-chair available for the invalid of Torsington-on-Sea, who, like myself, stands in need of the salubrious air of that health-giving resort, but who is ordered by his medical adviser to secure it with the least possible expenditure of physical strength.

Both Mr. Wisterwhistle and his chair are peculiar in their respective ways, and each has a decided

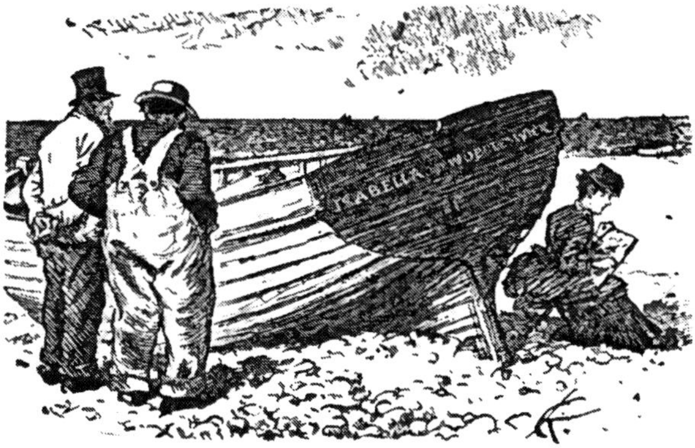

PERIL!

Gruff Voice (behind her—she thought she heard her own name). "She 's a gettin' old, Bill, and she sartain'y ain't no beauty! But you and I 'll smarten her up! Give her a good tarrin' up to the waist, and a streak o' paint, and they 'ont know her again when the folks come down a' Whitsun'. Come along, and let 's ketch 'old of her, and shove her into the water fust of all!!"

Miss Isabella. "Oh! the horrid wretches! No policeman in sight! Nothing for it but flight!" [*Is off like a bird!*

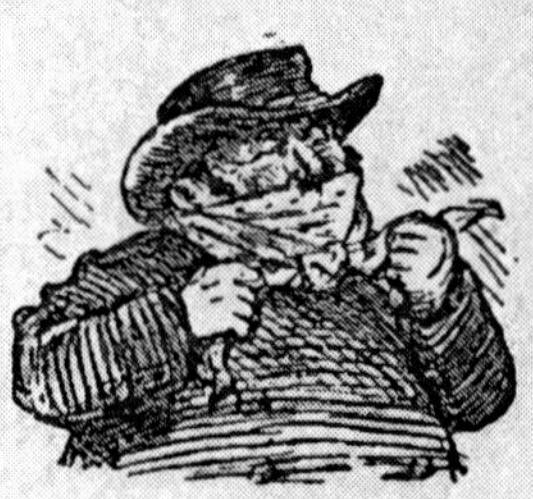

TYNEMOUTH

history. Mr. Wisterwhistle, growing confidential over his antecedents, says, "You see, sir, I wasn't brought up to the bath-chair business, so to speak, for I began in the Royal Navy, under His Majesty King William the Fourth. Then I took to the coastguard business, and having put by a matter of thirty pound odd, and hearing 'she' was in the market,"—Mr. Wisterwhistle always referred to his bath-chair as 'she,' evidently regarding it from the nautical stand-point as of the feminine gender,—"and knowing, saving your presence, sir, that old Bloxer, of whom I bought her, had such a good crop of cripples the last season or two, that he often touched two-and-forty shillings a week with 'em, I dropped Her Majesty's service, and took to this 'ere. But, Lor, sir, the business ain't wot it wos. Things is changed woeful at Torsington since I took her up. Then from 9 o'clock, as you might say, to 6 p.m., every hour was took up; and, mind you, by real downright 'aristocracy,'—real live

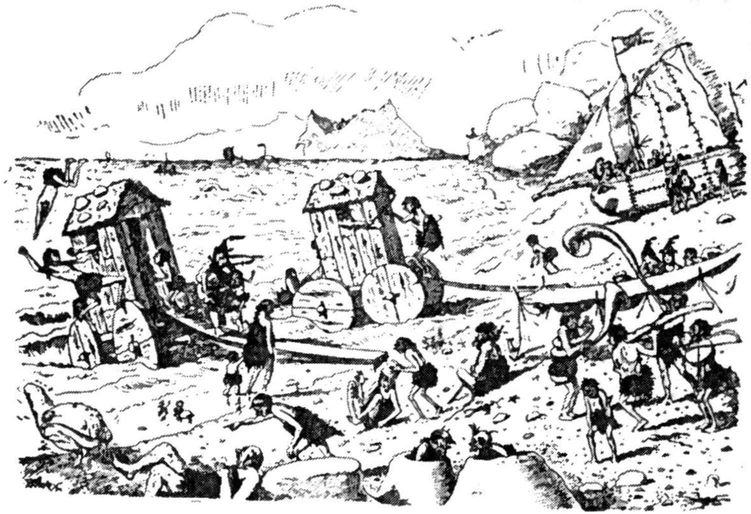

PREHISTORIC PEEPS

There were even then quiet spots by the sea where one could be alone with Nature undisturbed

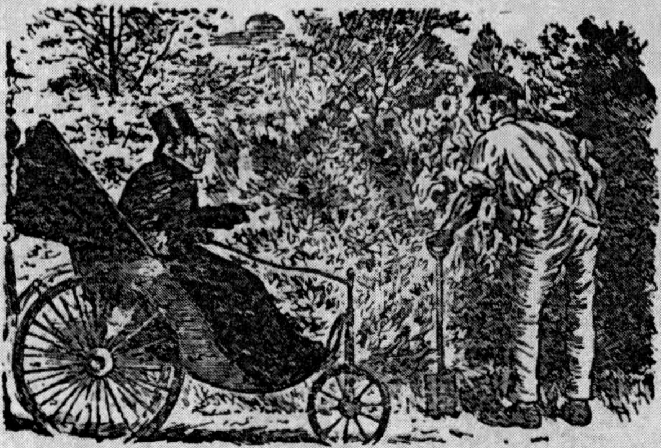

A SENSE OF PROPERTY

Botanical Old Gent (*in the Brighton Gardens*). "Can you tell me, my good man, if this plant belongs to the 'Arbutus' family?"

Gardener (*curtly*). "No, sir, it doan't. It b'longs to the Corporation!"

noblemen, with gout on 'em, as thought nothink of a two hours' stretch, and didn't 'aggle, savin' your presence, over a extra sixpence for the job either way. But, bless you, wot's it come to now? Why, she might as well lay up in a dry dock arf the week, for wot's come of the downright genuine invalid, savin' your presence, blow'd if I knows. One can see, of course, sir, in arf a jiffy, as you is touched in the legs with the rheumatics, or summat like it; but besides you and a old gent on crutches

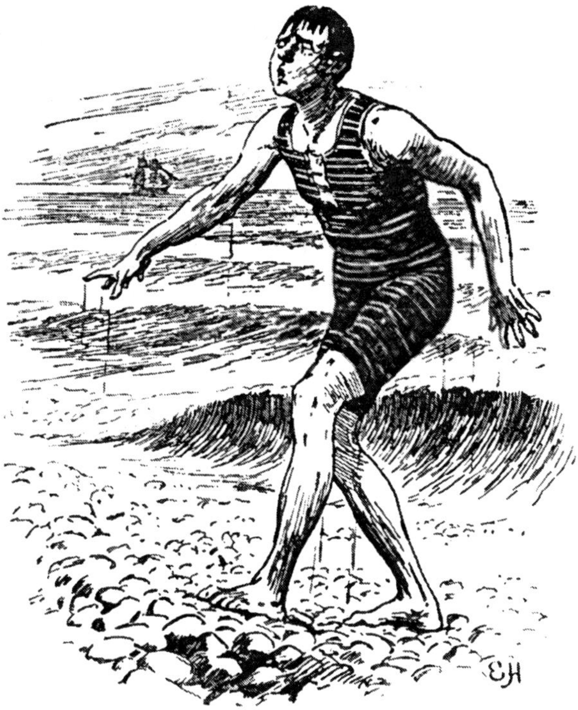

THE MINOR ILLS OF LIFE

Portrait of a gentleman attempting to regain his tent after the morning bath

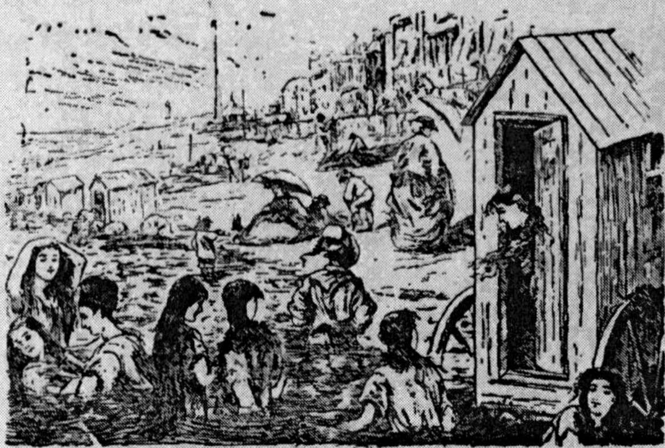

MERMAIDS' TOILETS IN '67

Blanche. "I say, some of you, call after aunty! She has taken my *chignon*, and left me her horrid black one!"

from Portland Buildings, there ain't no real invalid public 'ere at all, and one can't expect to make a livin' out of you two; for if you mean to do the thing ever so 'ansome, it ain't reasonable to expect you and the old gent I was a referring to, to stand seven hours a day goin' up and down the Esplanade between you, and you see even that at a bob an hour ain't no great shakes when you come to pay for 'ousing her and keepin' her lookin' spic and span, with all her brass knobs a shining and her leather apron fresh polished with patent carriage blackin': and Lor, sir, you'd not b'lieve me if I was to tell you what a deal of show some parties expects for their one bob an hour. Why, it was only the other day that Lady Glumpley (a old party with a front of black curls and yaller bows in her bonnet, as I dare say you've noticed me a haulin' up and

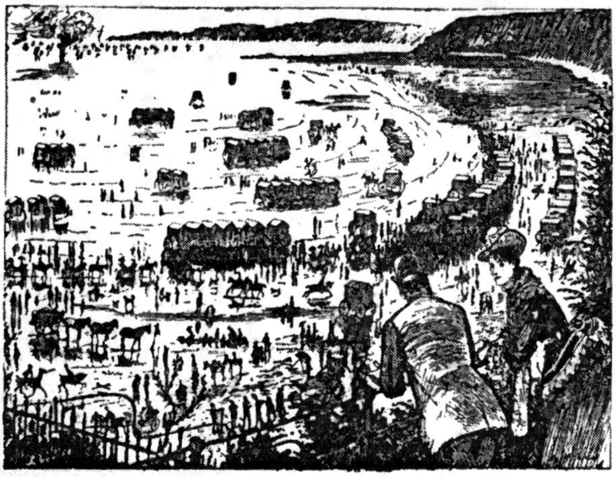

LOW TIDE ON SCARBOROUGH SANDS—BATHING UNDER DIFFICULTIES

The captain, who is well up in his classics, translates, for his Fanny's benefit, a celebrated Latin poem (by one Lucretius) to the effect that it is sweet to gaze from the cliff at the bathing machines vainly struggling to take the unfortunate bathers into deep water.

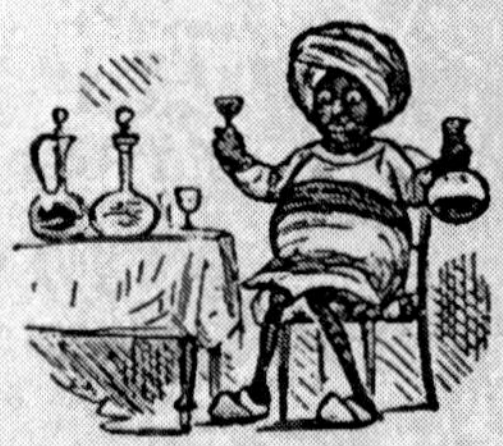

INDIAMAN GOING INTO PORT

down the Parade when the band's a playin'), says to me, says she, 'It ain't so much the easy goin' of your chair, Mr. Wisterwhistle, as makes me patronise it, as its general genteel appearance. For there's many a chair at Brighton that can't hold a candle to it!'" But at this point he was interrupted by the appearance of a dense crowd that half filled the street, and drew up in silent expectation opposite my front door. Dear me, I had quite forgotten I had sent for him. But the boy who cleans the boots and knives has returned, and brought with him *the One Policeman!*

QUERY AT SOME FASHIONABLE SEASIDE RESORT.—Do the unpleasant odours noticeable at certain times arise from the fact of the tide being high? If so, is the tide sometimes higher than usual, as the—ahem!—odours certainly are?

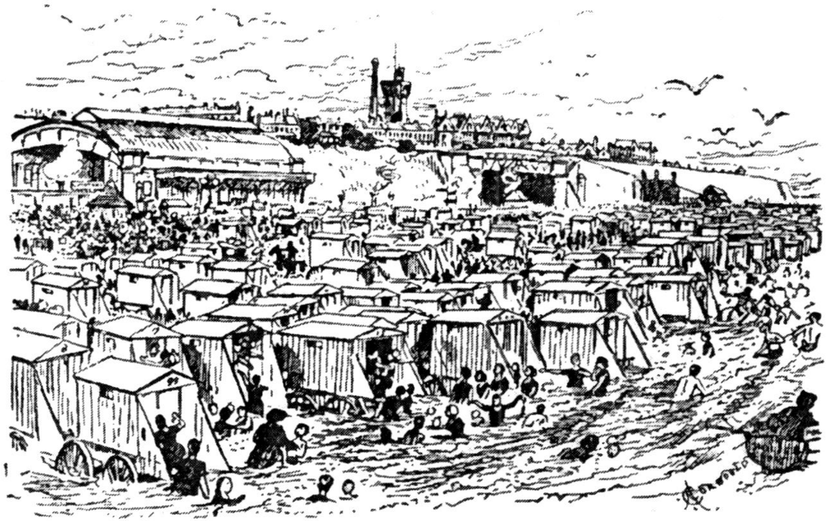

SEASIDE PUZZLE

To find your bathing-machine if you've forgotten the number

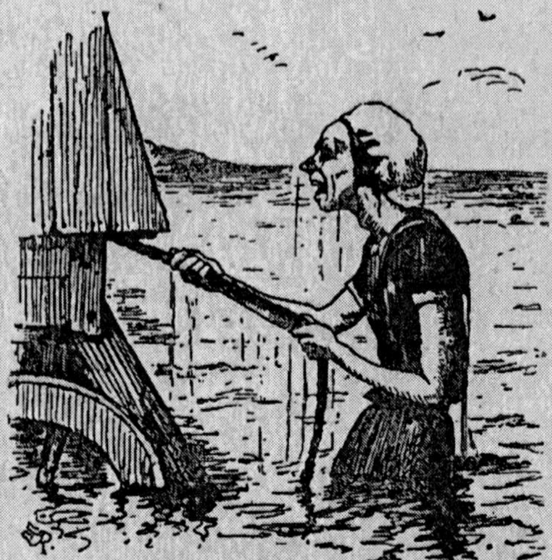

VENUS (ANNO DOMINI 1892) RISES FROM THE SEA!!

SEASIDE DRAMA.—*Mrs. de Tomkyns* (*sotto voce, to Mr. de T.*). "Ludovic, dear, there's Algernon playing with a strange child! *Do* prevent it!"

Mr. de T. (*ditto, to Mrs. de T.*). "How on earth am I to prevent it, my love?"

Mrs. de T. "Tell its parents Algernon is just recovering from scarlet fever, or something!"

Mr. de T. "But it isn't true!"

Mrs. de T. "Oh, never mind! Tell them, all the same!"

Mr. de T. (*aloud*). "Ahem! Sir, you'd better not let your little girl play with my little boy. He's only just recovering from—er—*Scarlet Fever!*"

Mr. and Mrs. Jenkins (*together*). "It's all right, sir!—*so's our little gal!*"

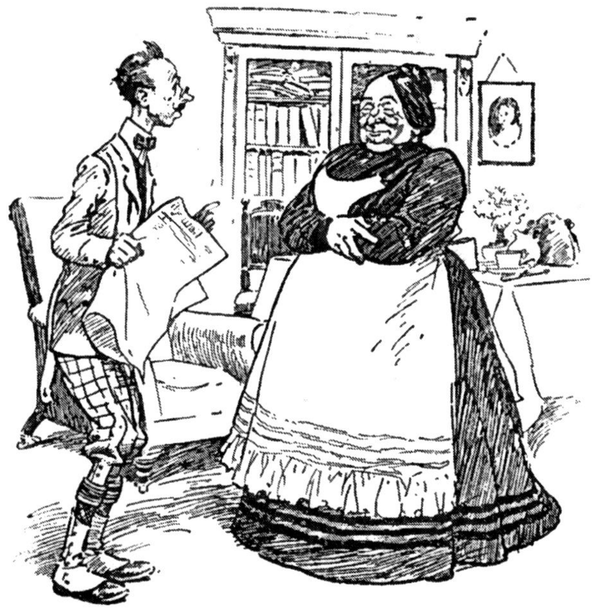

MIXED BATHING

Fussy Landlady (*to new Lodger*). "Well, sir, if you'll only tell me when you want a bath, *I'll see you have it.*"

BY THE SEASIDE

(*A Gasp and a Growl from Paterfamilias Fogey*)

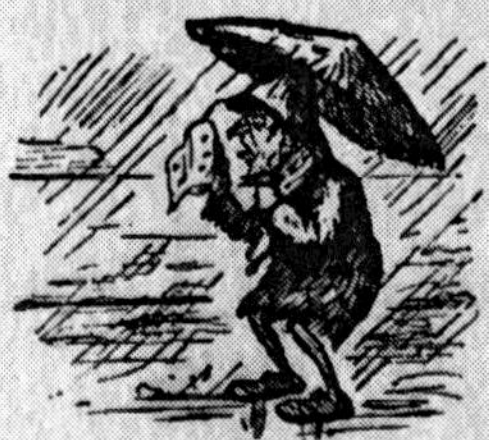

In for it here,
  Six weeks or more,
Once every year
  (Yah, what a bore!)
Daughters and wife
  Force me to bide
Mad to "see life"
  By the seaside!

Go out of town
  What if we do?
Hither comes down
  All the world too;
Vanity Fair,
  Fashion and Pride,
Seeking fresh air
  By the seaside.

Drest up all hands—
  Raiment how dear!—
Down on the sands,
  Out on the Pier,
Pace to and fro,
  See, as at Ryde,
Off how they show
  By the seaside!

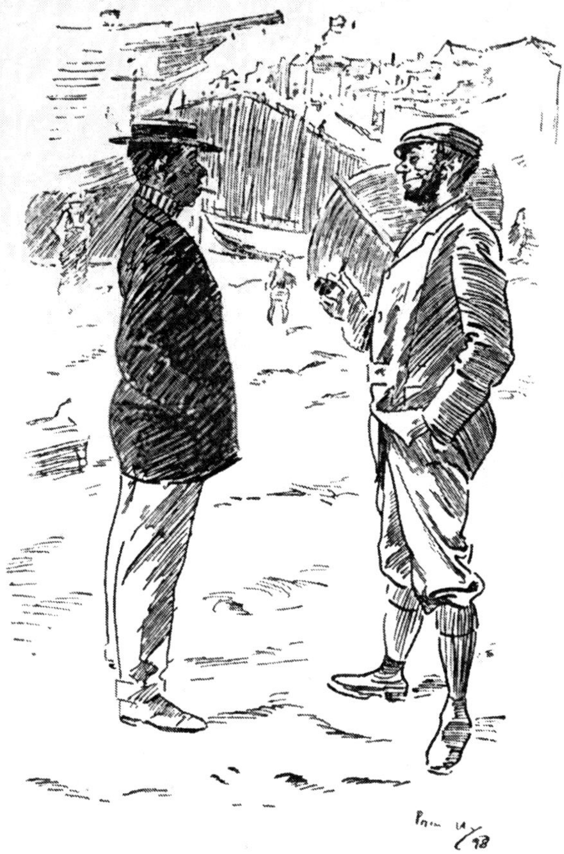

Snooks (*to new acquaintance*). "Tell yer what, look in one evenin' and 'ave a bit of supper, if you don't mind 'avin it in the kitchen. Yer see, we're plain people, and don't put on no side. Of course, I know as a toff like you 'ud 'ave it in the *drawing-room!*"

Mr. Punch at the Seaside

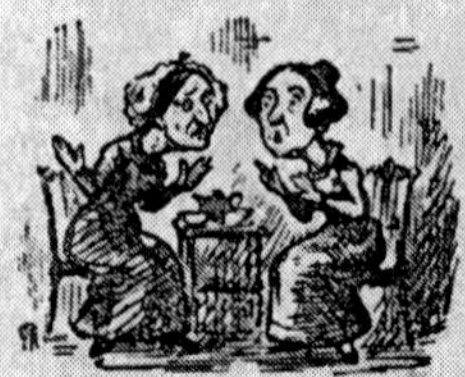

TORQUAY (TALKEY)

Fops and fine girls,
  Swarm, brisk as bees;
Ribbons and curls
  Float on the breeze;
Females and males
  Eye and are eyed;
Ogling prevails
  By the seaside!

Daughters may see
  Some fun in that.
Wife, how can she,
  Grown old and fat?
Scene I survey
  But to deride,
Idle display
  By the seaside.

Views within reach,
  Picturesque scenes,
Rocks on the beach,
  Bathing machines,
Shingle and pools,
  Left by the tide,
Youth, far from schools,
  By the seaside.

Artists may sketch,
  Draw and design,
Pencil, or etch;
  Not in my line.
Money, no end,
  Whilst I am tied
Here, I must spend,
  By the seaside!

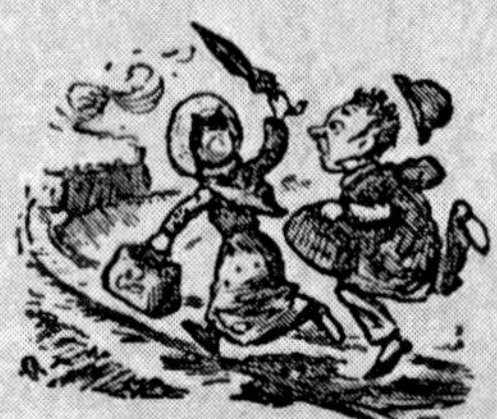

HASTINGS

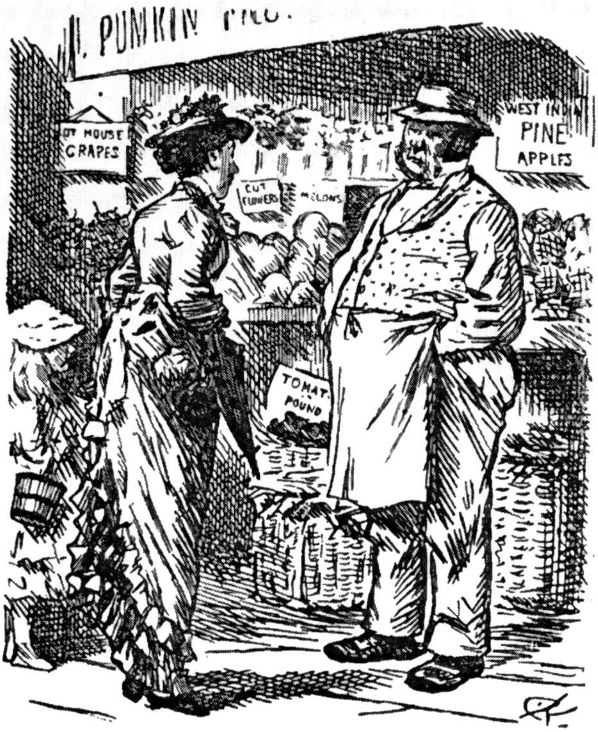

GENTILITY IN GREENS

Mrs. Brown finds Sandymouth a very different place from what she remembers it years ago.

Greengrocer. "Cabbage, mum !? We don't keep no second-class vegetables, mum. You'll get it at the lower end o' the town !"

SEASIDE VIEWS

KINGSWEAR

Tom Jones (*in love*). The most heavenly place I ever was in. The sun is warmer, the sky bluer, the sea the calmest I ever knew. Joy sparkles on every pebble; Art spreads its welcome arms through every spray of seaweed. True happiness encircles me on every breeze, and Beauty is by my side.

Old Jones. Beastly slow. All sea and sky, and ugly round stones. You can't bask in the sun because there is none—it's always raining—and because the flints worry your back. Confound the children, scraping up the wet sand and smelling seaweeds! It must be time for them to go to bed or to lessons or something. Wherever you sit there is sure to be a draught, and such heaps of old women you can't put your legs up on the

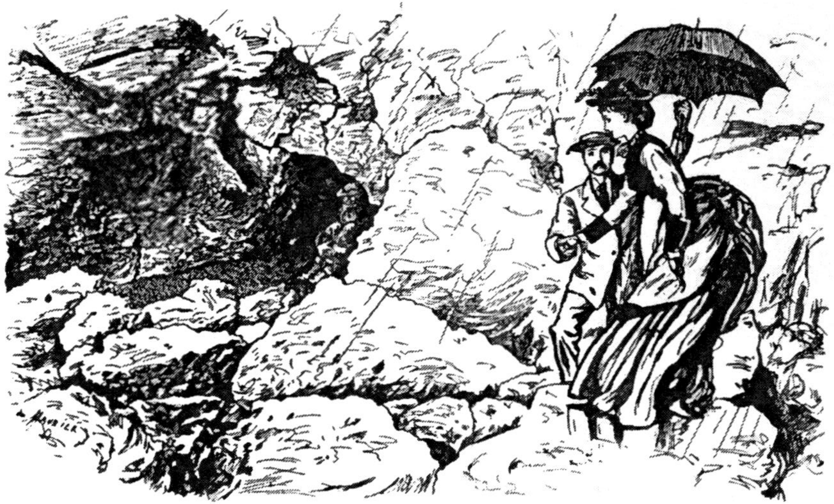

A FRAGMENT

Augustus knows a certain snug retreat—
A little rocky cavern by the sea—
Where, sheltered from the rain (and every eye),
He fondly hopes to breathe his tale of love
Into his artless Arabella's ear! . . . . .

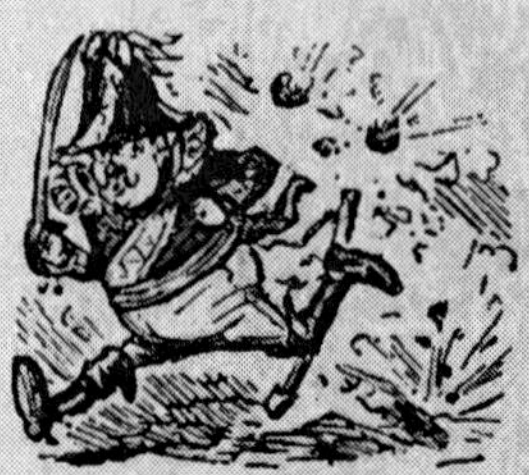

O-SHUN SHELLS!

seat. Hang it all, there isn't a young girl in the place, let alone pretty ones.

Young Brown (*waiting for a Commission*). Awfully dull. Quite too excessively detestable. Not a fellow to talk to, you know, who knows anything about the Leger, or draw-poker, or modern education, you know. Can't get introduced to Lady Tom Peeper. Nobody to do it. Wish my moustache would curl. Pull it all day, you know, but it won't come. Lady Tom smiled, on the Parade to-day. Got very red, but I shall smile too to-morrow. A man must do something in this dreadful place.

Major Brown (*Heavies*). Not half bad kind of diggings. Quite in clover. Found Lydia here—I mean Lady Tom Peeper. Horribly satirical woman, though. Keeps one up to the mark. I shall have to read up to keep pace with her. I shouldn't like to be chaffed by her. Better friend than enemy. Poor Tom Peeper! he must have a

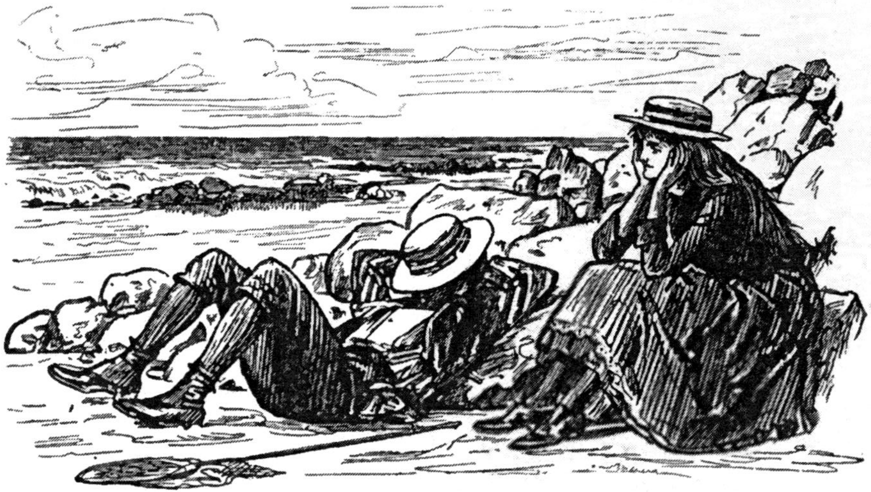

LONGING FOR A NEW SENSATION

Jack (*a naughty boy, who is always in disgrace, and most deservedly*). "I say, Effie, do you know what I should like? I should like to be accused of something I'd never done!"

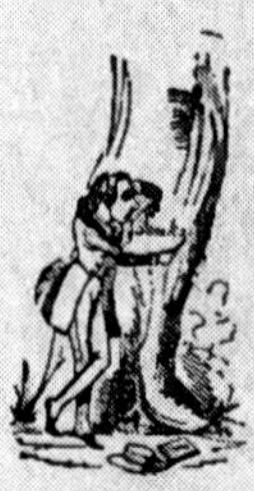

A CUTTER ON THE BEECH

bad time of it! Can't say "Bo" to a gosling. And she knows it. That's why he never comes down here. Coast clear. Fancy she's rather sweet on me. By Jove! we had a forty-mile-an-hour-express flirtation before her marriage! Must take care what I'm about now. Mustn't have a collision with Tom—good old man, after all, if he is a fool. Take this note round, Charles, to the same place.

Mrs. Robinson (*Materfamilias*). Scarcely room to swing a cot, for baby. Thank goodness, all the children are on the beach. I hope Mary Ann won't let out to the other nurses that Totty had the scarlet fever. He's quite well now, poor little man, and no one will be any the worse for it. Horrid! of course. No, it is not a Colorado beetle, Robinson. They infest the curtains; we did not bring them with us in our trunks. Do go out and buy some insect-powder, instead of looking stupid behind that nasty cigar. Oh, and get some soap and some tooth-powder, and order baby's tonic, and Jane's iron—mind, sesqui-sulphate of iron (I

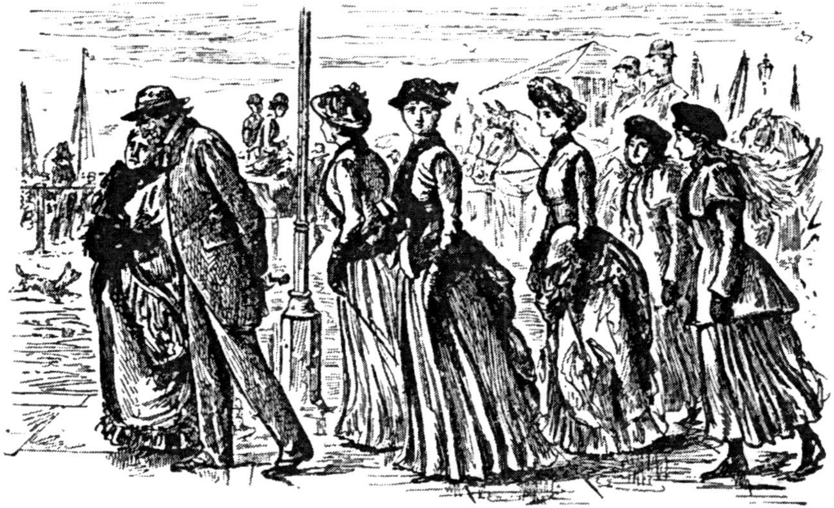

A LAMENT

Dowager. "It's been the worst season I can remember, Sir James! All the men seem to have got married, and none of the girls!"

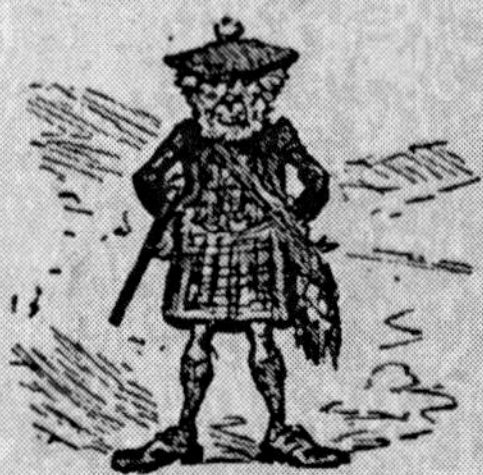

A SANDY COVE

suppose I must find the prescription), and a box of—what's that stuff for sore throats? And do hire a perambulator with a hood. And we have no dessert for to-morrow—you know, or you ought to know, it's Sunday. Some fruit, and what you like. Oh! and don't forget some biscuits for the dog. What has become of Tiny? Tiny! Tiny! I know he did not go with the children. I dare say he has eaten something horrid, and is dying under a chair. Dear! dear! who would be mother of a family with such a careless, thoughtless, quite too utterly selfish husband as you are. Of course you never remembered to-day was my birthday. I ought never to have been born. A bracelet or a pair of ear-rings—or, by the way, I saw a lovely châtelaine on the Parade. You might find enough to give me one pleasure since our wedding.

Robinson (*Paterfamilias*). I like the seaside, I do. When will it be over?

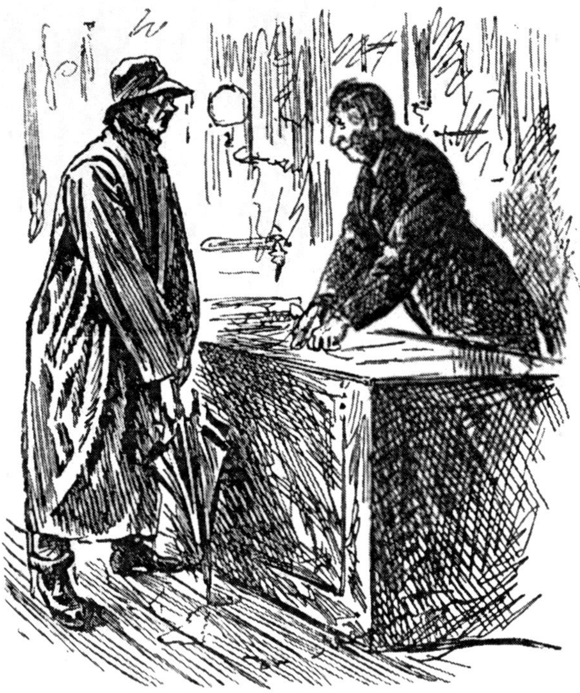

JOYS OF THE SEASIDE

Brown. "What beastly weather! And the glass is going steadily down!"

Local Tradesman. "Oh, that's nothing, sir. The glass has no effect whatever on *our* part of the coast!"

THE BETTER THE DAY, THE BETTER THE TALK !

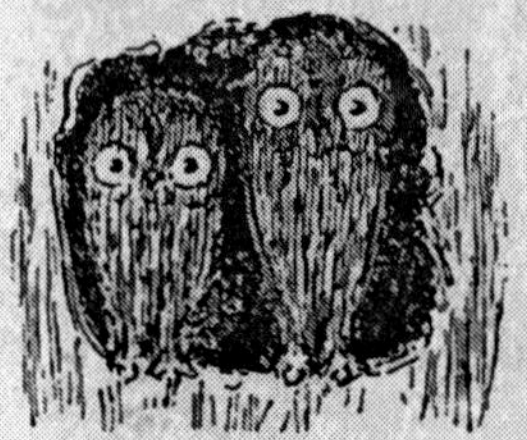

BROAD-STARES

SCENE—*Any fashionable Watering-place where "Church Parade" is a recognised institution.* TIME—*Sunday,* 1 P.M. *Enter* Brown *and* Mrs. Brown, *who take chairs.*

Mrs. Brown. Good gracious! Look another way! Those odious people, the Stiggingses, are coming towards us!

Brown. Why odious? I think the girls rather nice.

Mrs. B. (*contemptuously*). Oh, *you* would, because men are so easily taken in! Nice, indeed! Why, here's Major Buttons.

B. (*moving his head sharply to the right*). Don't see him! Can't stand the fellow! I always avoid him at the Club!

Mrs. B. Why? Soldiers are always such pleasant men.

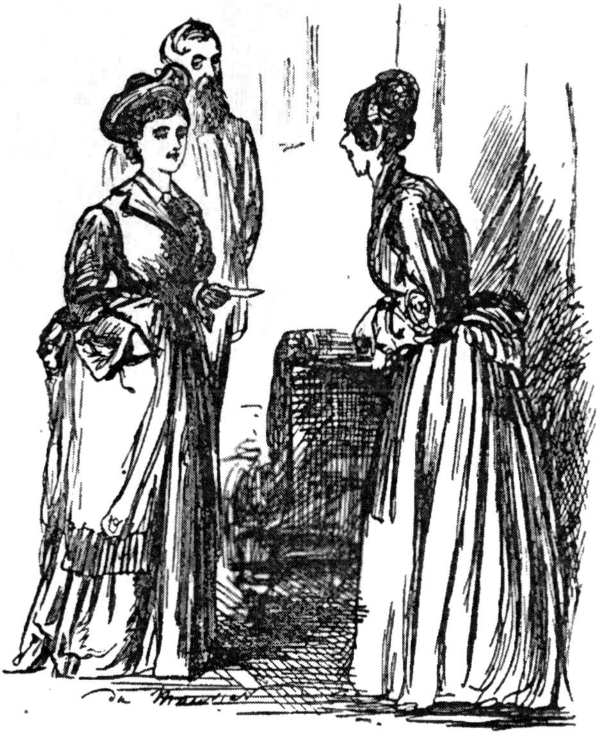

"BY THE SAD SEA WAVES"

Landlady (*who has just presented her weekly bill*). "I 'ope, ma'am, as you find the bracing hair agree with you, ma'am, and your good gentleman, ma'am!"

Lady. "Oh, yes, our appetites are wonderfully improved! For instance, at home we only eat two loaves a day, and I find, from your account, that we can manage eight!"

[*Landlady feels uncomfortable.*

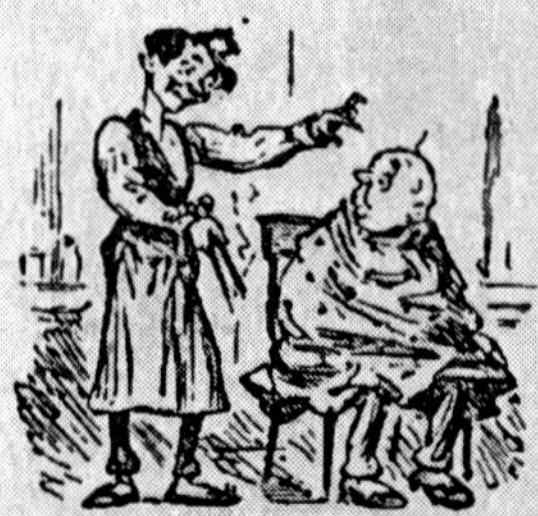

CURLEW

B. (*contemptuously*). Buttons a soldier! Years ago he was a Lieutenant in a marching regiment, and now holds honorary rank in the Volunteers! Soldier, indeed! Bless me! here's Mrs. Fitz-Flummery — mind you don't cut her.

Mrs. B. Yes, I shall; the woman is unsupportable. Did you ever see *such* a dress. And she has changed the colour of her hair—again!

B. Whether she has or hasn't, she looks particularly pleasing.

Mrs. B. (*drily*). You were always a little eccentric in your taste! Why, surely there must be Mr. Pennyfather Robson. How smart he looks! Where *can* he have come from?

B. The Bankruptcy Court! (*Drily.*) You were never particularly famous for discrimination. As I live, the Plantagenet Smiths!

[*He bows with effusion.*

Mrs. B. And the Stuart Joneses. (*She kisses her*

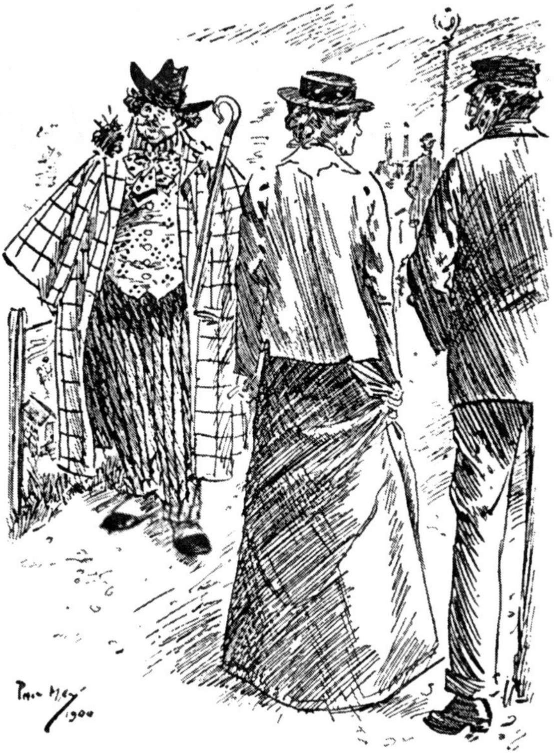

RATHER DIFFICULT

"Oh, I say, here comes that dismal bore, Bulkley! Let's pretend *we don't see him!*"

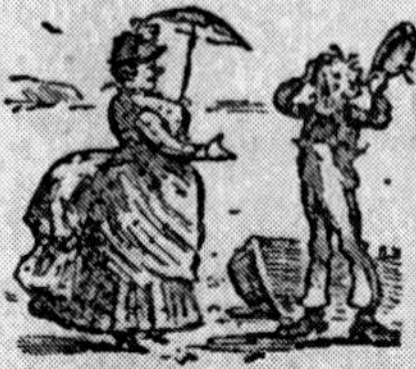

ROW ME O!

hand gushingly). By the way, dear, didn't you say that the Plantagenet Smiths were suspected of murdering their uncle before they inherited his property?

B. So it is reported, darling. And didn't you tell me, my own, that the parents of Mr. Stuart Jones were convicts before they became millionaires?

Mrs. B. So I have heard, loved one. (*Starting up.*) Come, Charley, we must be off at once! The Goldharts! If they catch us, *she* is sure to ask me to visit some of her sick poor!

B. And *he* to beg me to subscribe to an orphanage or a hospital! Here, take your prayer-book, or people won't know that we have come from church! [*Exeunt hurriedly.*

AT SCARBOROUGH.—*Miss Araminta Dove.* Why do they call this the Spa?

Mr. Rhino-Ceros. Oh! I believe the place was once devoted to boxing exhibitions.

[*Miss A. D. as wise as ever.*

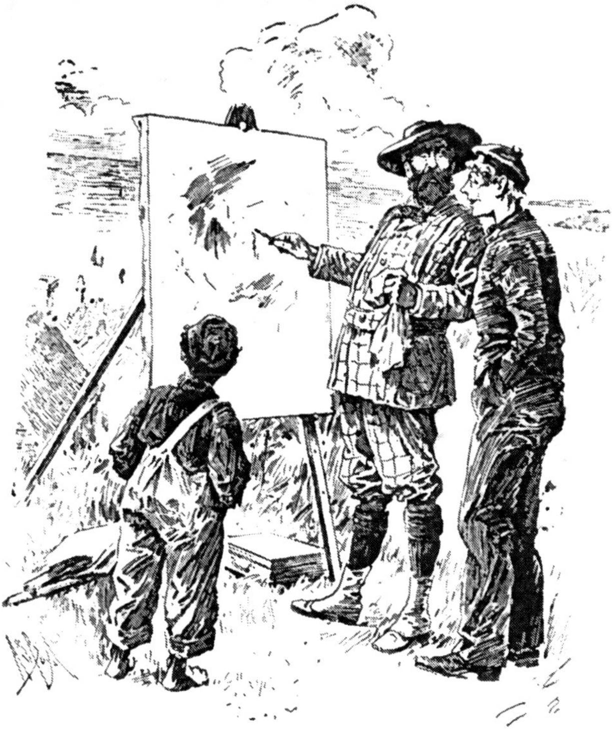

PESSIMISM

Artist (*irritated by the preliminaries of composition and the too close proximity of an uninteresting native*). "I think you needn't wait any longer. There's really nothing to look at just now."

Native. "Ay, an' I doot there'll *never* be muckle to look at there!"

THE DONKEY-BOYS OF ENGLAND

(*A Song for the Seaside*)

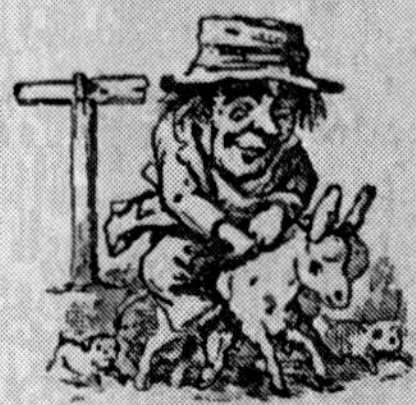

THE Donkey-Boys of England, how merrily they fly,
With pleasant chaff upon the tongue and cunning in the eye.
And oh! the donkeys in a mass how patiently they stand,
High on the heath of Hampstead, or down on Ramsgate's sand.

The Donkey-Boys of England, how sternly they reprove
The brute that won't "come over," with an impressive shove;
And oh! the eel-like animals, how gracefully they swerve
From side to side, but won't advance to spoil true beauty's curve.

The Donkey-Boys of England, how manfully they fight,
When a probable donkestrian comes suddenly in sight;
From nurse's arms the babies are clutch'd with fury wild,
And on a donkey carried off the mother sees her child.

The Donkey-Boys of England, how sternly they defy
The pleadings of a parent's shriek, the infant's piercing cry;
As a four-year-old MAZEPPA is hurried from the spot,
Exposed to all the tortures of a donkey's fitful trot.

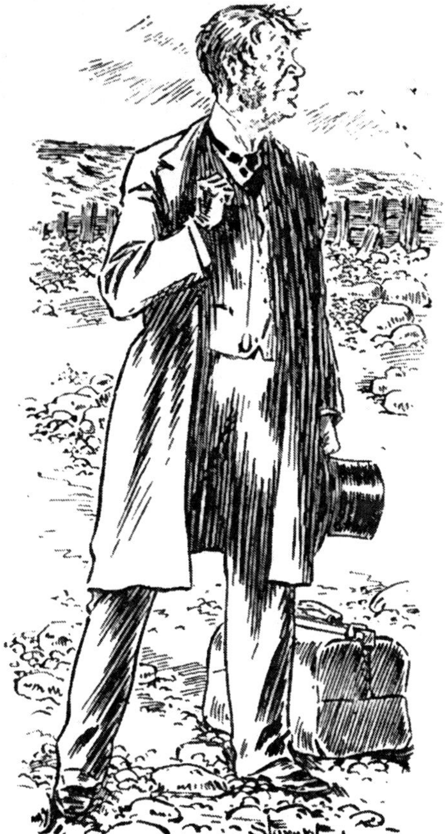

Portrait of a gentleman who sent his wife and family to the seaside, followed by a later train, and left their address behind. [*Sketched after five hours' futile search for them.*

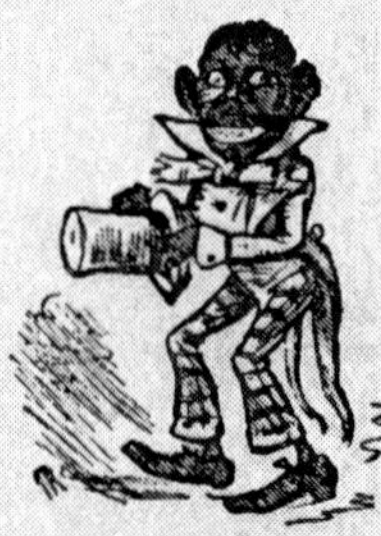

THE JETTY

The Donkey-Boys of England, how
lustily they scream,
When they strive to keep together
their donkeys in a team;
And the riders who are anxious to be
class'd among genteels,
Have a crowd of ragged Donkey-boys
"hallooing" at their heels.

The Donkey-Boys of England, how
well they comprehend
The animal to whom they act as
master, guide, and friend;
The understanding that exists between them who'll dispute—
Or that the larger share of it falls sometimes to the brute?

SEASIDE ACQUAINTANCES (SCENE—The Shady Side of Pall Mall).—*Snob.* My Lord, you seem to forget me. Don't you recollect our meeting this summer at Harrogate?

Swell. My dear fellow, I do not forget it in the least. I recollect vividly we swore eternal friendship at Harrogate, and should it be my fate to meet you at Harrogate next year, I shall only be too happy to swear it again.

[*Lifts his chapeau, and leaves Snob in a state of the most speechless amazement.*

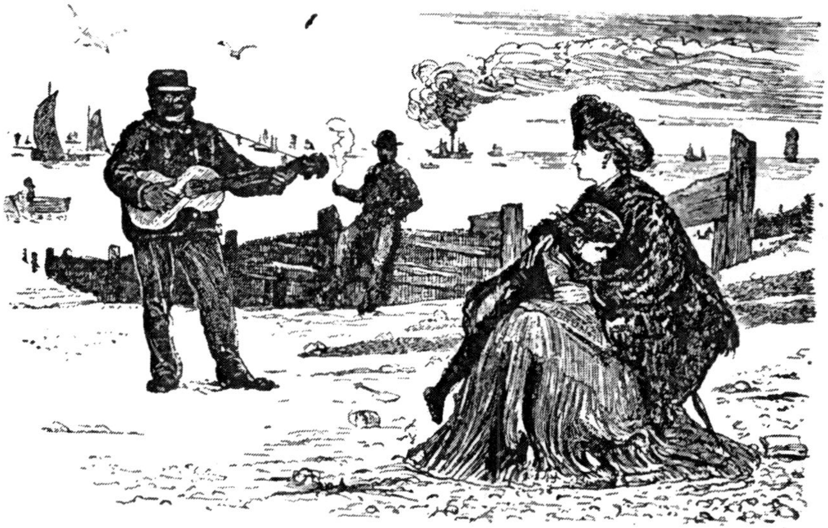

A VOICE FROM THE SEA

"O let me kiss him for his mother!"

REASONS FOR GOING TO BRIGHTON

(By the Cynic who stays in London)

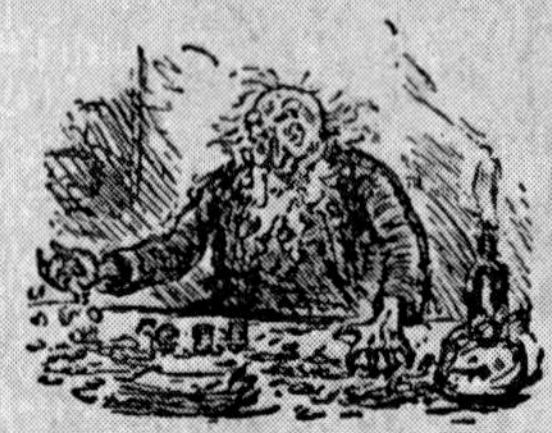

"HA! RICH!"

BECAUSE "everybody" is there, and it is consequently so pleasant to see St. John's Wood, Bayswater, and even Belgravia, so well represented on the Esplanade.

Because the shops in the King's Road are *nearly* as good as those to be found in Regent Street.

Because the sea does not *always* look like the Thames at Greenwich in a fog.

Because some of the perambulating bands play very nearly in tune.

Because the Drive from the Aquarium to the New Pier is quite a mile in length, and only grows monotonous after the tenth turn.

Because watching fish confined in tanks is such rollicking fun.

Because the Hebrews are so numerously represented on the Green.

Because the Clubs are so inexpensive and select.

Because the management of the Grand is so very admirable.

Because it is so pleasant to follow the Harriers on a hired hack in company with other hired hacks.

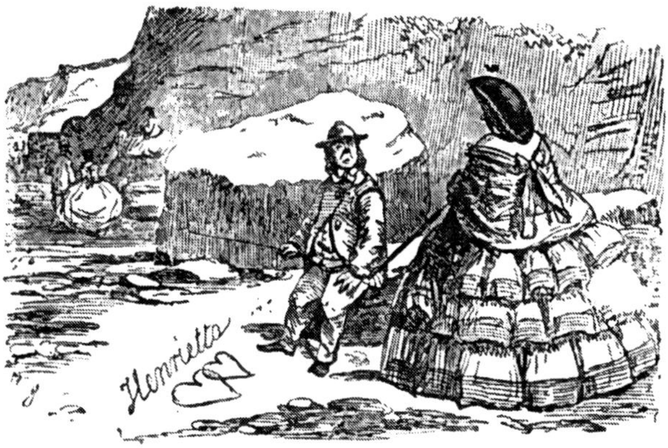

SCENE—BY THE SAD SEA WAVES

Tomkins, disconsolate on a rock, traces some characters upon the sand. To him, Mrs. Tomkins (whose name is Martha).

Mrs. T. "Well, Mr. Tomkins, and pray who may Henrietta be?"

[*Tomkins utters a yell of despair, and falls prostrate.*

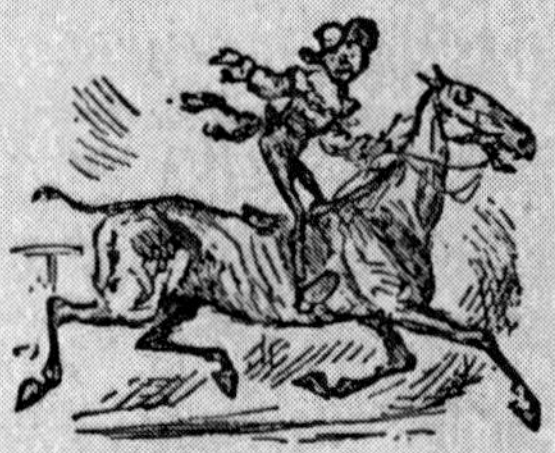

WESTON-SUPER-MARE

Because the half-deserted Skating Rinks are so very amusing.

Because it is so nice to hear second-rate scandal about third-rate people.

Because the place is not always being visited by the scarlet fever.

Because it is so cheerful to see the poor invalids taking their morning airing in their bath-chairs.

Because the streets are paraded by so many young gentlemen from the City.

Because the Brighton belles look so ladylike in their quiet Ulsters and unpretending hats.

Because the suburbs are so very cheerful in the winter, particularly when it snows or rains.

Because on every holiday the Railway Company brings down such a very nice assortment of excursionists to fill the streets.

Because Brighton in November is so very like Margate in July.

Because, if you did not visit Brighton, you might so very easily go farther and fare worse.

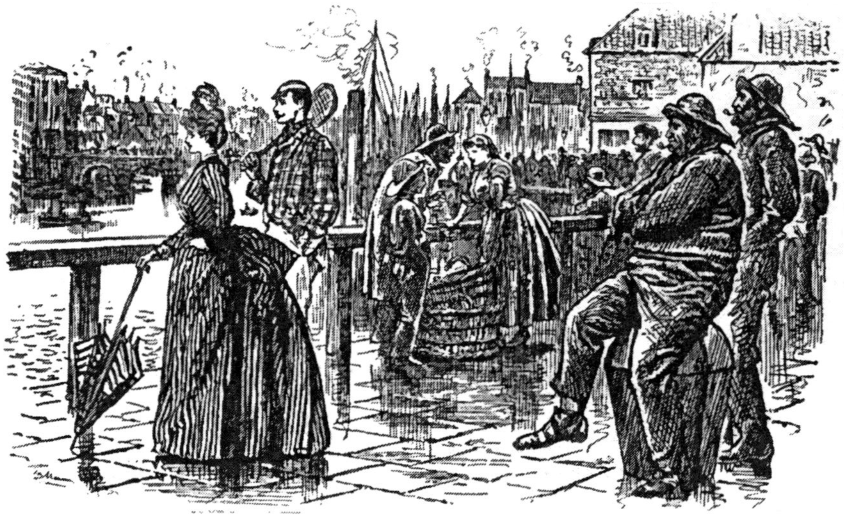

A VIKING ON MODERN FASHION

"What does t'lass want wi' yon *boostle* for? It aren't big enough to *smoggle* things, and she can't *steer* herself wi' it!"

THE TRIPPER

(*By a Resident*)

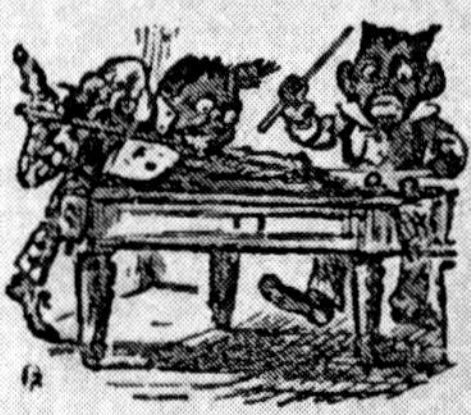

BLACKPOOL

WHAT does he come for?
 What does he want?
Why does he wander thus
 Careworn and gaunt?
Up street and down street with
 Dull vacant stare,
Hither and thither, it
 Don't matter where?

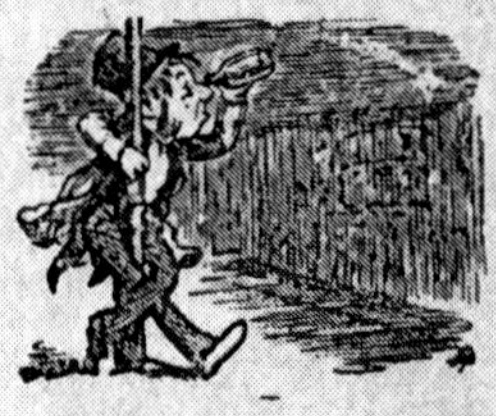

BRIGHTON

What does he mean by it?
 Why does he come
Hundreds of miles to prowl,
 Weary and glum,
Blinking at Kosmos with
 Lack-lustre eye?
He doesn't enjoy it, he
 Don't even try!

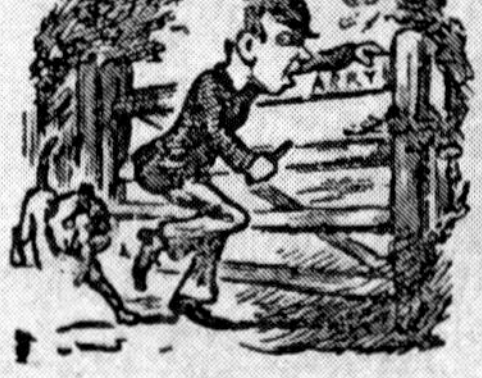

MARGATE

Sunny or soaking, it's
 All one to him,
Wandering painfully—
 Curious whim!
Gazing at china-shops,
 Gaping at sea,
Guzzling at beer-shops, or
 Gorging at tea.

Why don't he stay at home,
  Save his train fare,
Soak at his native beer,
  Sunday clothes wear?
No one would grudge it him,
  No one would jeer.
Why does he come away?
  Why is he here?

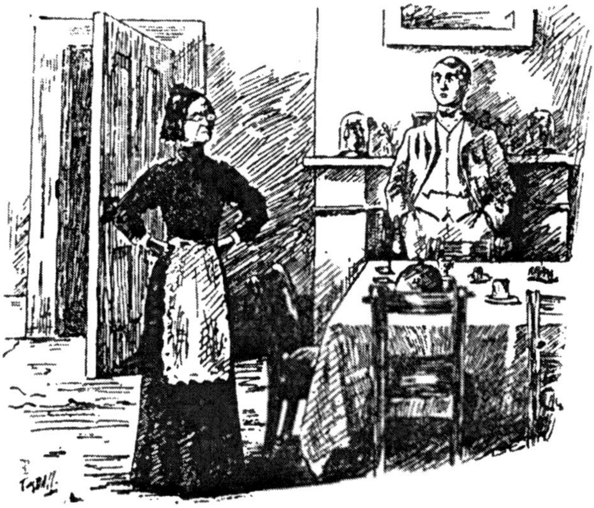

A SLIGHT MISUNDERSTANDING

Landlady. "I hope you slept well, sir?"

New Boarder. "No, I didn't. I've been troubled with insomnia."

Landlady. "Look here, young man. I'll give you a sovereign for every one you find in that bed!"

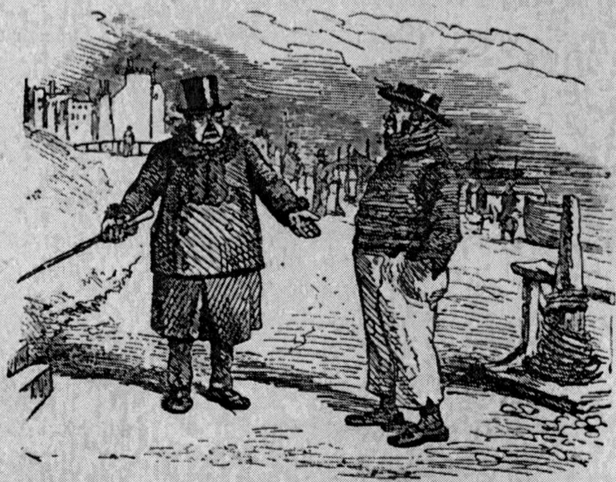

TOUCHING APPEAL

Testy Old Gent. (*wearied by the importunities of the Brighton boatmen*). "Confound it, man! Do I *look* as if I wanted a boat?"

ROBERT AT THE SEASIDE

I'VE bin spending my long Wacation of a fortnite at Northgate.

Northgate's a nice quiet place, Northgate is, tho' it quite fails in most things that constitoots reel injoyment at the seaside, such as Bands and Niggers and Minstrels and all that.

It's a grand place for weather, for it generally blows hard at Northgate, and wen it doesn't blow hard it rains hard, which makes a nice change, and a change is wot we all goes to the sea-side for.

It seems a werry favrite place for inwaleeds, for the place is full on 'em, Bath cheers is in great demand and all the seats on the Prade is allus occypied by 'em.

Dr. Scratchem too sends most of his favrite cases

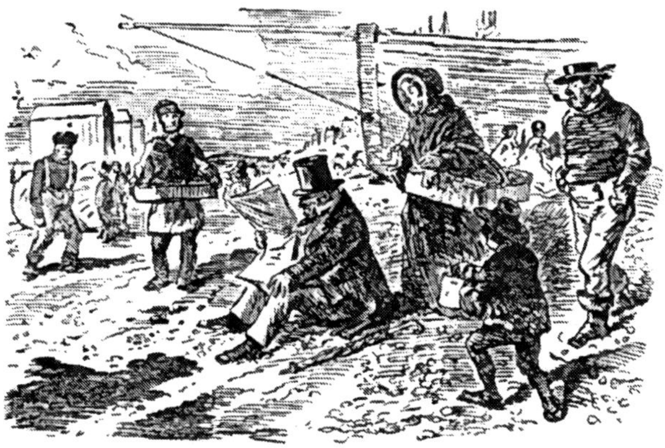

THE BORES OF THE BEACH

So! as it's a fine day, you'll sit on the beach and read the paper comfortably, will you? Very good! Then we recommend you to get what guinea-pigs, brandy-balls, boats, and children's socks, to say nothing of shell-workboxes, lace collars, and the like you may want, before you settle down.

there, and you can't walk on the Peer without facing lots on 'em.

Brown says the place makes him as sollem as a Common Cryer, and he hasn't had a good hearty larf since he came here, but then Brown isn't quite sattisfied with his Lodgings, and has acshally recommended his Land Lady to turn her house into the Norfolk Howard Hotel, *Unlimited*, so

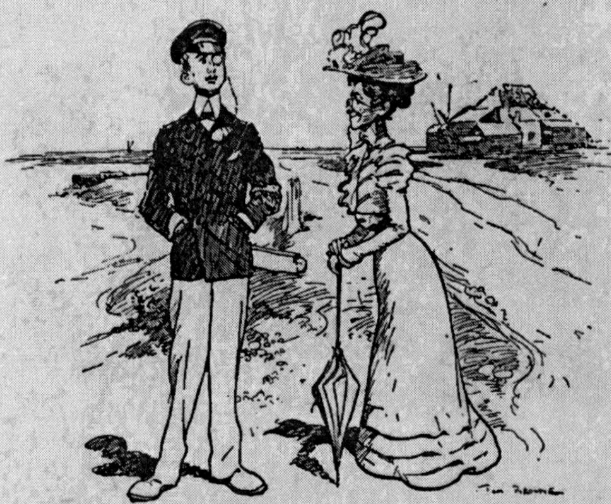

"Excuse me, sir. I seem to have met you before. Are you not a relative of Mr. Dan Briggs?"
"No, madam. I *am* Mr. Dan Briggs himself."
"Ah, then that explains the remarkable resemblance!"

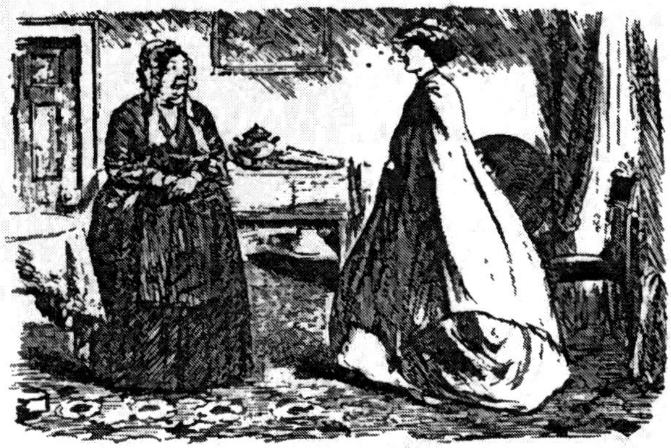

ACCOMMODATING

Lodger. "And then, there's that cold pheasant, Mrs. Bilkes"——

Landlady. "Yes'm, and if you should have enough without it, lor', Mr. Bilkes wouldn't mind a eatin' of it for his supper, if that's all."

perhaps she may account for his want of spirits. Northgate's rather a rum place as regards the tide. Wen it's eye it comes all over the place and makes such a jolly mess, and wen it's low it runs right out to sea and you can't see it. Brown tried to persuade me as how as one werry eye tide was a spring tide, but as it was in September I wasn't so green as to beleeve that rubbish.

It seems quite a pet place for Artists, I mean Sculpchers, at least I s'pose they must be Sculpchers,

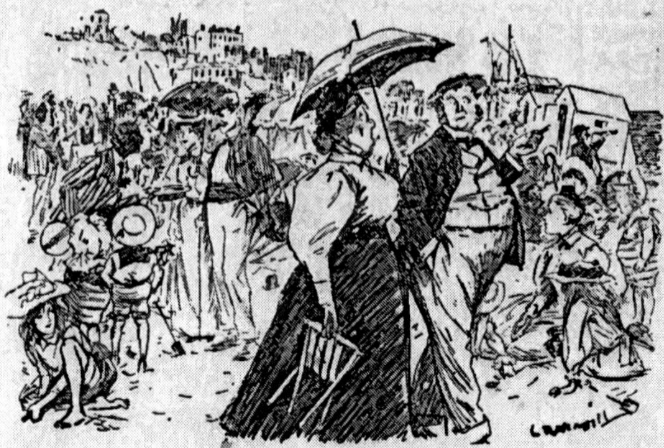

Mrs. Brown. "Might I ask how much you gave that nigger?"

Mr. Brown (*first day down*). "Sixpence."

Mrs. B. "Oh, indeed! Perhaps, sir, you are not aware that your wife and family have listened to those same niggers for the last ten days for a *penny!*"

and that they brings their Moddels with 'em, for the Bathing Machines is stuck close to the Peer, so dreckly after breakfast the Moddels goes and bathes in the Sea, and the Sculpchers goes on the Peer, and there's nothink to divert their attention from their interesting studdys, and many on 'em passes ours there quietly meditating among the Bathing Machines.

Brown says, in his sarcastic way, it's the poor Sculpchers as comes here, who can't afford to pay for their Moddels, so they comes here and gets 'em free gratis for nothink.

There's sum werry nice walks in the nayberhood but I never walks 'em, for it seems to me that the grate joke of every Buysicler and Trysicler, and the place swarms with 'em, is to cum quietly behind you and see how close he can go by you without nocking you down. I'm sure the jumps

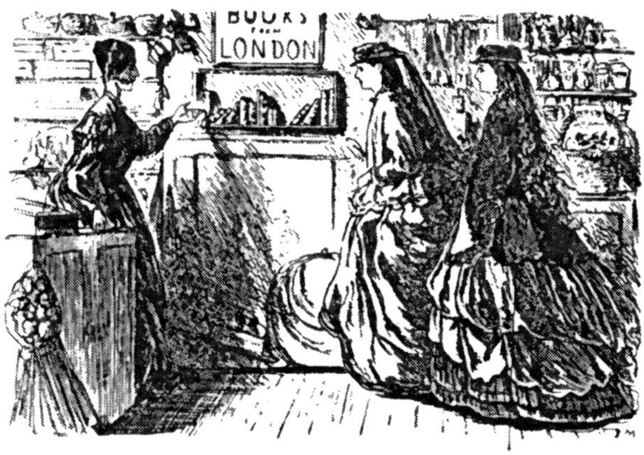

PLEASURES OF THE SEASIDE

Mermaiden. "I am told you keep a circulating library?"

Librarian. "Yes, miss. *There* it is! Subscription, two shillings a-week; one volume at a time; change as often as you please! Would you like to see a catalogue?"

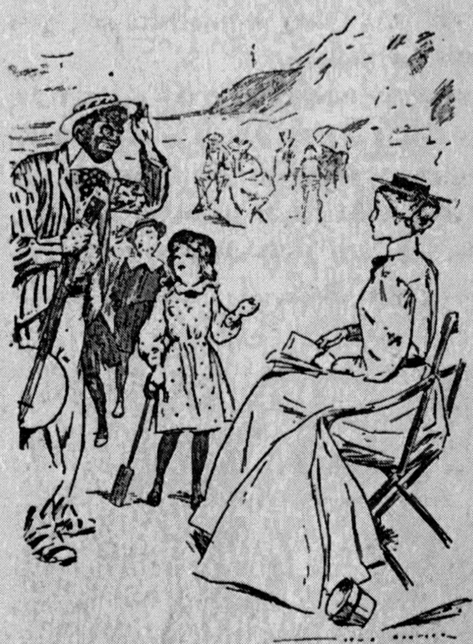

AN INFORMAL INTRODUCTION

Polite Little Girl (*suddenly*). "This is my mamma, sir. Will you please sing her, 'It's the seasoning wot does it!'"

and the starts and the frites as I had the fust day or too kep my Art in my mouth till I thort it would have choked me.

How Ladys, reel Ladys too, can expose theirselves on such things I can't make out. I herd a young Swell say that wot with them and what with the Bathing Moddels it was as good as a Burlesk!

We've got werry cumferrabel Lodgings, we have, just opposite the Gas Works and near a Brick Field. When the wind is South or West we smells the bricks and when its East we smells the Gas, but when its doo North we don't smell nuffen excep just a trifle from the Dranes, and so long as we keeps quite at the end of the werry long

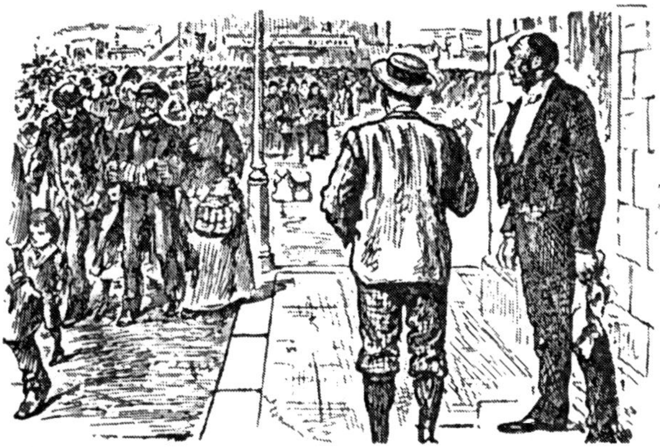

OUT OF TOWN

(UNFASHIONABLE INTELLIGENCE)

Visitor. "What a roaring trade the hotels will be doing with all these holiday folk!"

Head waiter at The George. "Lor bless yer, sir, no! They all bring their nosebags with 'em!"

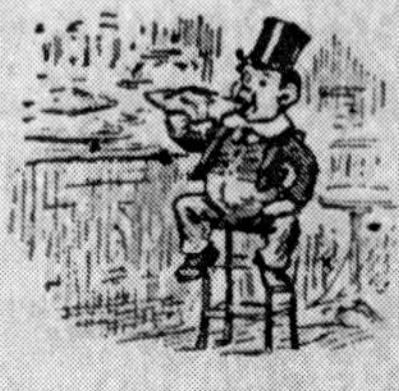

LIGHT PUFFS RAISED A LITTLE SWELL

Peer we don't smell nuffen at all excep the sea weed.

Our Landlord's a werry respeckabel man and the Stoker on our little Railway, and so werry fond of nussing our little children that they are allus as black as young Sweeps. Their gratest treat is to go with him to the Stashun and stand on the ingin when they are shuntin, so preshus little they gits of the sea breezes.

We've had a fust rate Company staying here. I've seen no less than 2 Aldermen, and 1 Warden of a City Compny, but they didn't stay long. I don't think the living was good enuff for 'em. It must be a werry trying change, from every luxery that isn't in season, to meer beef and mutton and shrimps! and those rayther course.

I think our Boatmen is about the lazyest set of fellows as ever I seed. So far from begging on you to have a soft Roe with the Tide, or a hard Roe against it, they makes all sorts of egscewses for not taking you, says they're just a going to dinner, or they thinks the wind's a gitting

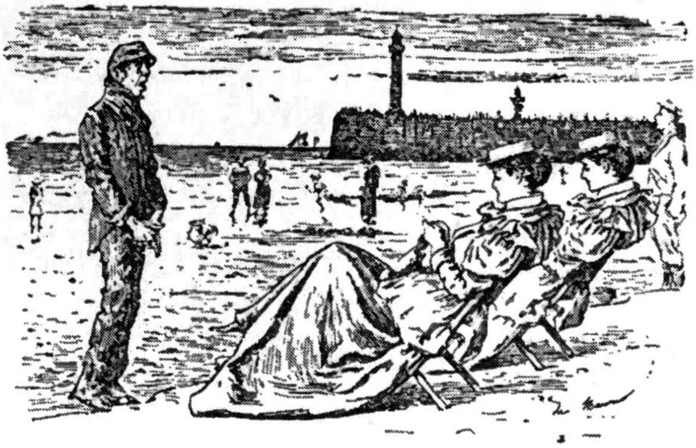

SEASIDE STUDIES

Wandering Minstrel. "Gurls! I'm a doocid fine cha-appie!" &c., &c.

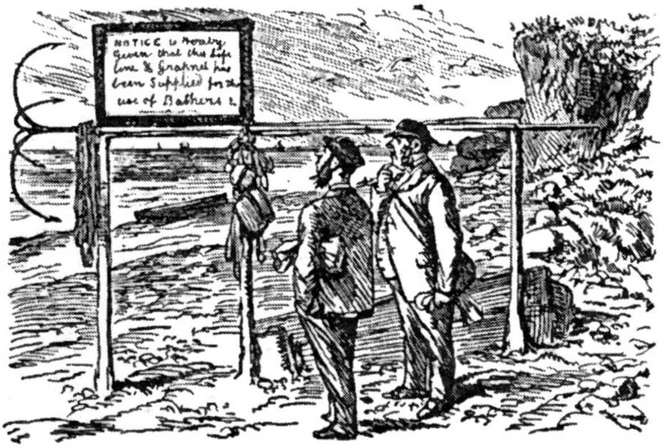

Wiggles and Sprott prefer bathing from the beach to having a stuffy machine. They are much pleased with the delicate little attention indicated above!

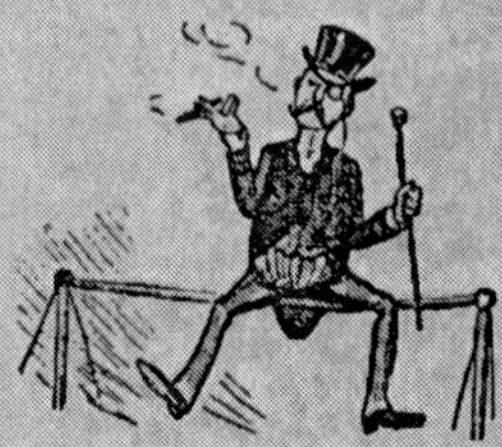

HEAVY SWELL ON THE BAR

up, or there ain't enough water!

Not enuff water in the Sea to flote a Bote! wen any one could see as there was thousands of galluns there.

I saw some on 'em this mornin bringin in sum fish, and asked the price of a pair of Souls, but they axshally said they didn't dare sell one, for every man Jack of 'em must be sent to Billingsgate! but werry likely sum on 'em might be sent back again in the arternoon, and then I could get some at the Fishmonger's!

What a nice derangemunt!

There was the butiful fresh fish reddy for eating, there was me and my family reddy to eat 'em, but no, they must be packed in boxes and carried to the Station and then sent by Rale to London, and then sent by Wan to Billingsgate, and that takes I'm told ever so many hours, and then carried back to the London Stashun, and then sent by Rale to Northgate, and then carried from the Stashun to

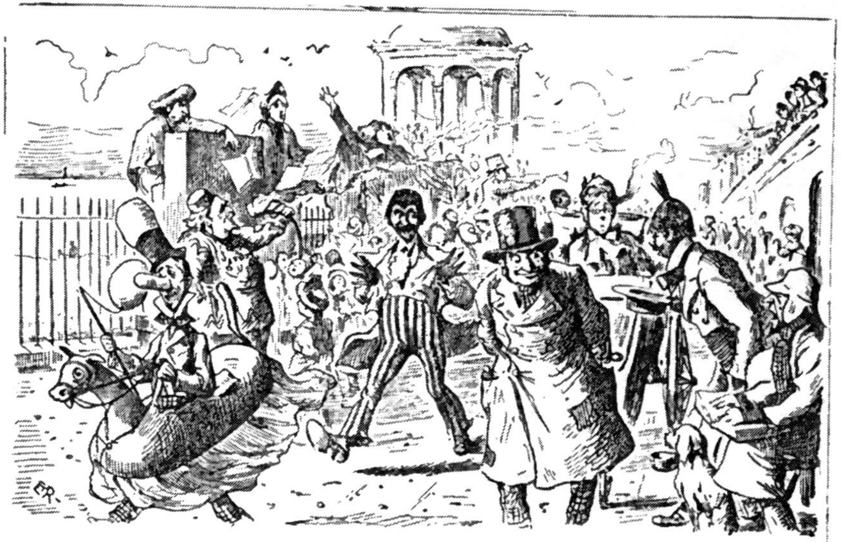

A QUIET DRIVE BY THE SEA

A Brighton bath-chairman's idea of a suitable route for an invalid lady

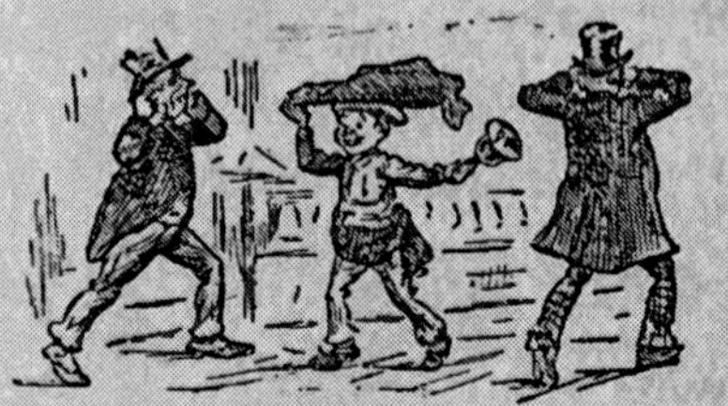

THE BELL BUOY

the Fishmonger's, and then I'm allowed to buy 'em!

Well if that isn't a butiful business like arrangement, my Lord Mare, I should like to know what is.

However, as I wunce herd a Deputy say, when things cums to their wust, things is sure to mend, and I don't think that things can be much wusser than that.

(*Signed*) ROBERT.

THE SPIRIT OF THE THING.—*Landlady* (*to shivering lodger*). No, sir, I don't object to your dining at a restorong, nor to your taking an 'apenny paper, but I must resent your constant 'abit of locking up your whiskey, thereby himplying that me, a clergyman's daughter, is prone to larceny.

[*Lodger immediately hands her the key as a guarantee of good faith.*

A SEASIDE ROUNDEL

On the sands as loitering I stand
Where my point of view the scene commands,
I survey the prospect fair and grand
On the sands.

Niggers, half a dozen German bands,
Photographic touts, persistent, bland,
Chiromancers reading dirty hands,

Nursemaids, children, preachers, skiffs that land
Trippers with cigars of fearful brands,
Donkeys—everything, in short, but sand—
On the sands.

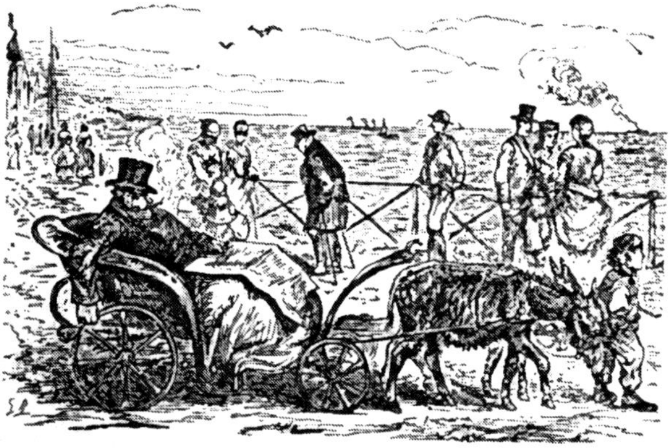

THE LETTER BUT NOT THE SPIRIT

Old Mr. de Cramwell, being bilious and out of sorts, is ordered to go to the sea, and take plenty of exercise in the open air. (He begins at once.)

COMMON OBJECTS OF THE SEASHORE

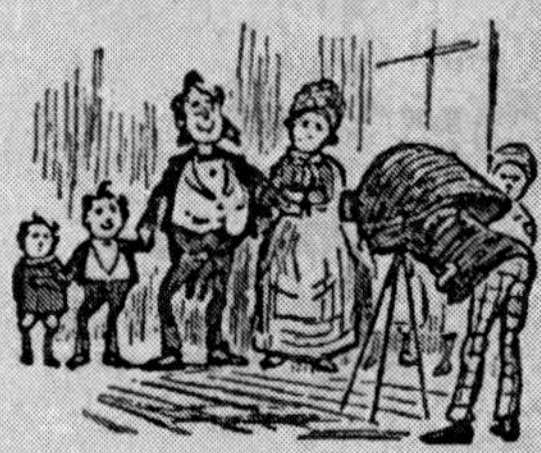

TAKING A ROW

THE "disguised minstrel," believed by the public to be a peer of the realm collecting coin for a charity, but who is in reality the sentimental singer from a perambulating troop of nigger banjoists, "working on his own."

The preacher whose appreciation of the value of logic and the aspirate is on a par.

The intensely military young man whose occupation during eleven months in the year is the keeping of ledgers in a small city office.

The artist who guarantees a pleasing group of lovers for sixpence, frame included.

The band that consists of a cornet, a trombone, a clarionet, some bass, and a big drum, which is quite as effective (thanks to the trombone) when all the principals have deserted in search of coppers.

And last (and commonest of all) the cockney who, after a week's experience of the discomforts of the seaside, is weary of them, and wants to go home.

A WINDY CORNER AT BRIGHTON

(By an Impressionist)

OLD lady first, with hair like winter snows,
Makes moan.
And struggles. Then, with cheeks too richly rose,
A crone,
Gold hair, new teeth, white powder on her nose;
All bone
And skin; an "Ancient Mystery," like those
Of Hone.
Then comes a girl; sweet face that freshly glows!
Well grown.
The neat cloth gown her supple figure shows
Now thrown
In lines of beauty. Last, in graceless pose,
Half prone,
A luckless lout, caught by the blast, one knows
His tone
Means oaths; his hat, straight as fly crows,
Has flown.
I laugh at him, and—— Hi! By Jove, there goes
My own!

ON THE SANDS

(*A Sketch at Margate*)

Close under the Parade wall a large circle has been formed, consisting chiefly of Women on chairs and camp-stools, with an inner ring of small Children, who are all patiently awaiting the arrival of a troupe of Niggers. At the head of one of the flights of steps leading up to the Parade, a small and shrewish Child-nurse is endeavouring to detect and recapture a pair of prodigal younger Brothers, who have given her the slip.

Sarah (*to herself*). Wherever can them two plegs have got to? (*Aloud; drawing a bow at a venture.*) Albert! 'Enery! Come up 'ere this minnit. *I* see yer!

'Enery (*under the steps—to Albert*). I say—d'ye think she *do?*—'cos if——

Albert. Not she! Set tight. [*They sit tight.*

Sarah (*as before*). 'Enery! Albert! You've bin and 'alf killed little Georgie between yer!

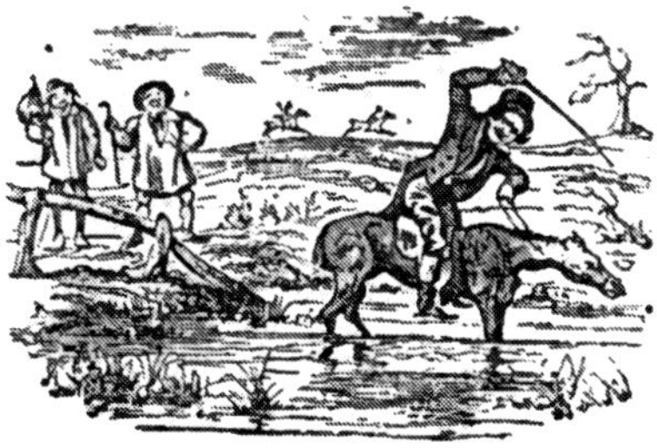

STOPPING AT A WATERING PLACE

'Enery (*moved, to Albert*). Did you 'ear that, Bert? It wasn't *me* upset him—was it now?

Albert (*impenitent*). 'Oo cares? The Niggers'll be back direckly.

Sarah. Al-bert! 'Enery! Your father's bin down 'ere once after you. You'll *ketch* it!

Albert (*sotto voce*). Not till father ketches *us*, we shan't. Keep still, 'Enery—we're all right under 'ere!

Sarah (*more diplomatically*). 'Enery! Albert! Father's bin and left a 'ap'ny apiece for yer. Ain't yer comin' up for it? If yer don't want it, why, stay where you are, that's all!

Albert (*to 'Enery*). I *knoo* we 'adn't done nothin'. An' I'm goin' up to git that 'ap'ny, I am.

'Enery. So 'm I.

[*They emerge, and ascend the steps—to be pounced upon immediately by the ingenious Sarah.*

Sarah. 'Ap'ny, indeed! You won't git no

'apence *'ere*, *I* can tell yer—so jest you come along 'ome with me!

[*Exeunt Albert and 'Enery, in captivity, as the Niggers enter the circle.*

Bones. We shall commence this afternoon by 'olding our Grand Annual Weekly Singing Competition, for the Discouragement of Youthful Talent. Now then, which is the little gal to step out first and git a medal? (*The Children giggle, but remain seated.*) Not one? Now I arsk *you*—What *is* the use o' me comin' 'ere throwin' away thousands and thousands of pounds on golden medals, if you won't take the trouble to stand up and sing for them? Oh, you'll make me so wild, I shall begin spittin' 'alf-sovereigns directly—I *know* I shall! (*A little Girl in a sun-bonnet comes forward.*) Ah, 'ere's a young lady who's bustin' with melody, *I* can see. Your name, my dear? Ladies and Gentlemen, I have the pleasure to announce that Miss Connie Cockle will now appear. Don't curtsey till the Orchestra gives the chord. (*Chord from the harmonium—the Child advances, and curtsies with much aplomb.*) Oh, lor! call *that* a curtsey—that's a *cramp*, that is!

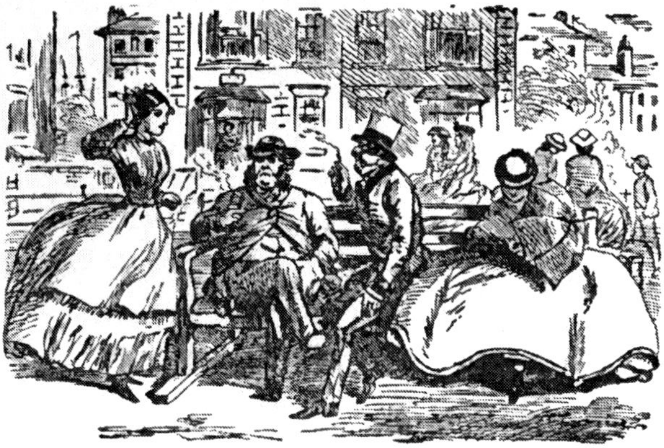

THE LAST DAY AT THE SEASIDE—PACKING UP

Maid (*to Paterfamilias*). "Please, sir, missus say you're to come in, and sit on the boxes; because we can't get 'em to, and they wants to be corded."

Do it all over again! (*The Child obeys, disconcerted.*) That's *worse!* I can see the s'rimps blushin' for yer inside their paper bags! Now see Me do it. (*Bones executes a caricature of a curtsey, which the little Girl copies with terrible fidelity.*) That's *ladylike*—that's genteel. Now sing *out!* (*The Child sings the first verse of a popular music-hall song, in a squeaky little voice.*) Talk about nightingales! Come 'ere, and receive the reward for extinguished incapacity. On your knees! (*The little Girl kneels before him while a*

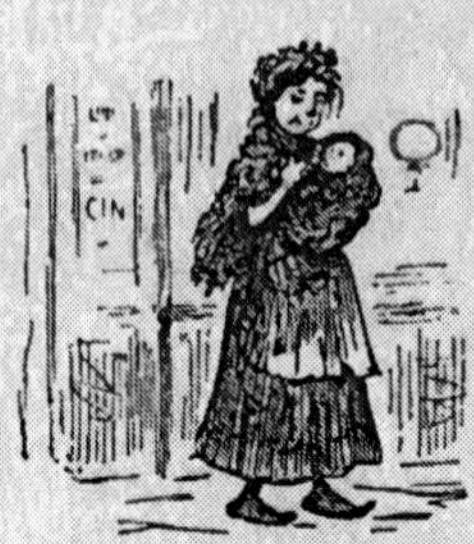

EAST-BORN

tin medal is fastened upon her frock.) Rise, Sir Connie Cockle! Oh, you *lucky* girl!

[*The Child returns, swelling with triumph, to her companions, several of whom come out, and go through the same performance, with more or less squeakiness and self-possession.*

First Admiring Matron (*in audience*). I do like to see the children kep' out o' mischief like this, instead o' goin' paddling and messing about the sands!

Second Ad. Mat. Just what *I* say, my dear—they're amused and edjucated 'ow to beyave at the same time!

First Politician (*with the "Standard"*). No, but look here—when Gladstone was asked in the House whether he proposed to give the Dublin Parliament the control of the police, what was his answer. Why . . . .

The Niggers (*striking up chorus*). "'Rum-tumty diddly-umty doodah-dey! Rum-tumty-diddly-um was all that he could say. And the Members and the Speaker joined together in the lay. Of 'Rum-tumty-diddly-umty doodah-dey!'"

Second Pol. (*with the "Star"*). Well, and what more would you have '*ad* him say? Come, now!

Alf (*who has had quite enough ale at dinner—to his fiancée*). These Niggers ain't up to much, Loo. Can't sing for *nuts!*

Chorley (*his friend, perfidiously*). You'd better go in and show 'em how, old man. Me and Miss

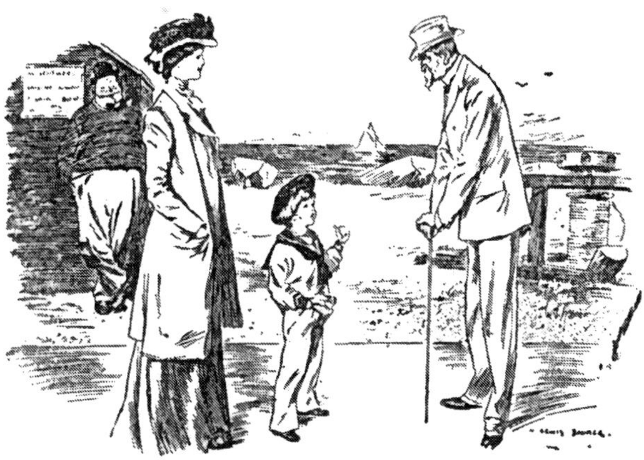

The General. "And what are you going to be when you grow up, young man?"

Bobbie. "Well, I can't quite make up my mind. I don't know which would be nicest—a soldier, like you, or a sailor, like Mr. Smithers."

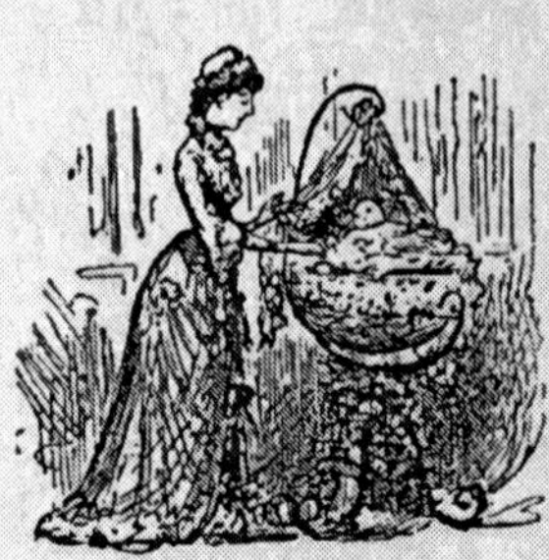

WEST-BORN

Serge'll stay and see you take the shine out of 'em!

Alf. P'raps you think I can t. But, if I was to go upon the 'Alls now, I should make my fortune in no time! Loo's 'eard me when I've been in form, and she'll tell you——

Miss Serge. Well, I will say there's many a professional might learn a lesson from Alf—whether Mr. Perkins believes it or not.

[*Cuttingly, to* "*Chorley.*"

Chorley. Now reelly, Miss Loo, don't come down on a feller like that. I want to see him do you credit, that's all, and he couldn't 'ave a better opportunity to distinguish himself—now *could* he?

Miss Serge. I'm not preventing him. But I don't know—these Niggers keep themselves very select, and they might object to it.

Alf. I'll soon square *them.* You keep your eye on me, and I'll make things a bit livelier!

[*He enters the circle.*

Miss Serge (*admiringly*). He *has* got a cheek, I

must say! Look at him, dancing there along with those two Niggers—they don't hardly know what to make of him yet!

Chorley. Do you notice how they keep kicking him beyind on the sly like? I wonder he puts up with it!

Miss S. He'll be even with them presently—you see if he isn't.

[*Alf attempts to twirl a tambourine on his finger, and lets it fall; derision from audience; Bones pats him on the head and takes the tambourine away—at which Alf only smiles feebly.*

Chorley. It's a pity he gets so 'ot dancing, and he don't seem to keep in step with the others.

Miss S. (*secretly disappointed*). He isn't used to doing the double-shuffle on sand, that's all.

The Conductor. Bones, I observe we have a recent addition to our company. Perhaps he'll favour us with a solo. (*Aside to Bones.*) 'Oo *is* he? 'Oo let him in 'ere—*you*?

Bones. I dunno. I thought *you* did. Ain't he stood nothing?

Conductor. Not a brass farden!

Bones (*outraged*). All right, you leave him to me. (*To Alf.*) Kin it be? That necktie! them familiar

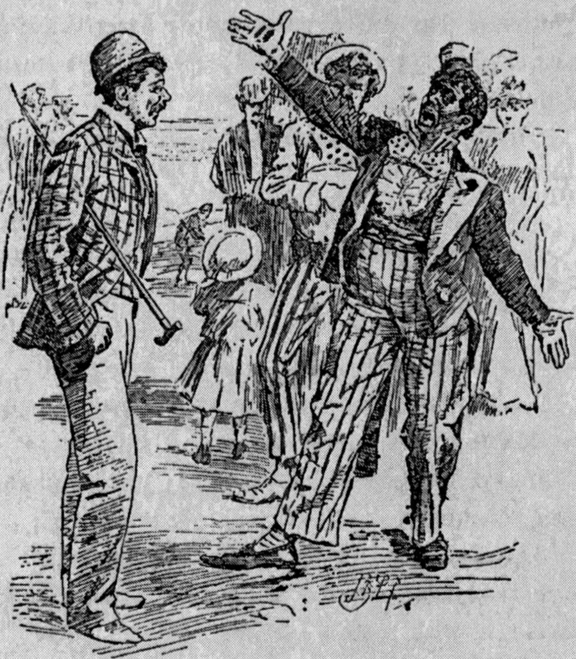

coat-buttons! that paper-dicky! You are—you *are* my long-lost convick son, 'ome from Portland! Come to these legs! (*He embraces Alf, and smothers him with kisses.*) Oh, you've been and rubbed off some of your cheek on my complexion—you *dirty* boy! (*He playfully "bashes" Alf's hat in.*) Now show the comp'ny how pretty you can sing. (*Alf attempts a music-hall ditty, in which he, not unnaturally, breaks down.*) It ain't my son's fault, Ladies and Gentlemen, it's all this little gal in front here, lookin' at him and makin'

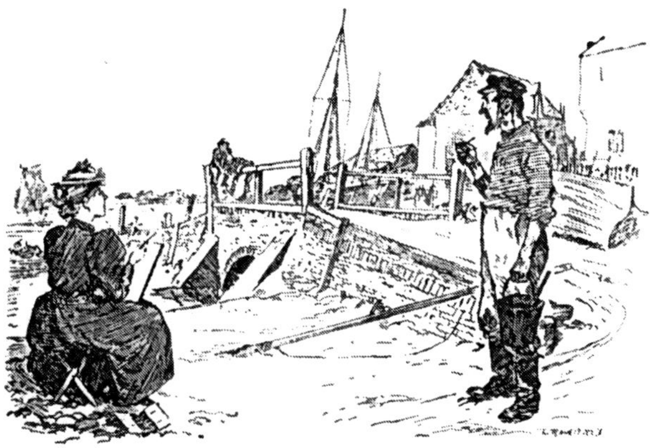

"THEM ARTISES!"

Lady Artist. "Do you belong to that ship over there?"
Sailor. "Yes, miss."
Lady Artist. "Then would you mind loosening all those ropes? They are much too tight, and, besides, I can't draw straight lines!"

him shy! (*To a small Child, severely.*) You oughter know *worse*, you ought! (*Clumps of seaweed and paper-balls are thrown at Alf, who by this time is looking deplorably warm and foolish.*) Oh, what a popilar fav'rite he is, to be sure!

Chorley (*to Miss S.*). Poor fellow, he ain't no match for those Niggers—not like he is now! Hadn't I better go to the rescue, Miss Loo?

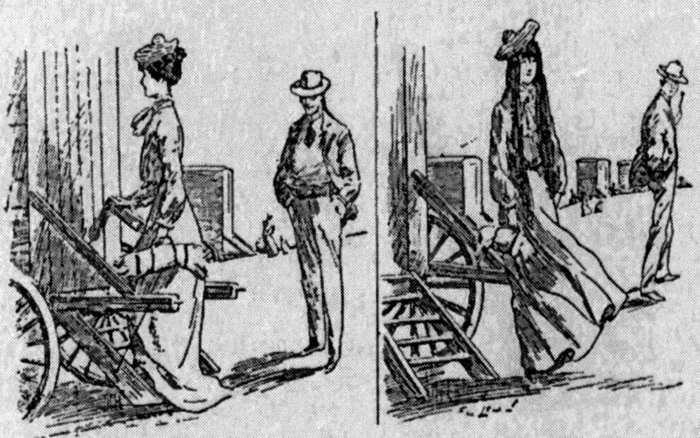

THE DISORDER OF THE BATH

How Belinda Brown appeared with "waves all over her hair" before taking a bath in the sea—and | How she looked after having some more "waves all over it."

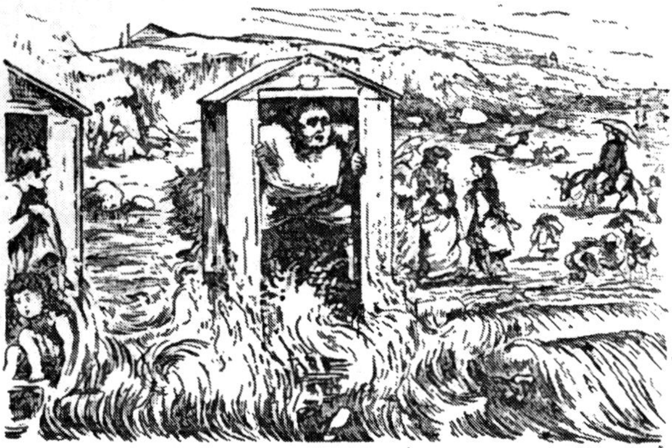

CAUTION TO BATHERS

Don't let them jolt you up the beach till you are dressed.

Jones (*obliged to hold fast*). "Hullo! Hi! Somebody stop my boots!"

Miss S. (*pettishly*). I'm sure I don't care *what* you do.

["*Chorley*" *succeeds, after some persuasion, in removing the unfortunate Alf.*

Alf (*rejoining his fiancée with a grimy face, a smashed hat, and a pathetic attempt at a grin*). Well? I *done* it, you see!

Miss S. (*crushingly*). Yes, you *have* done it! And the best thing you can do now, is to go home and wash your face. *I* don't care to be seen about with a *laughing-stock*, I can assure you!

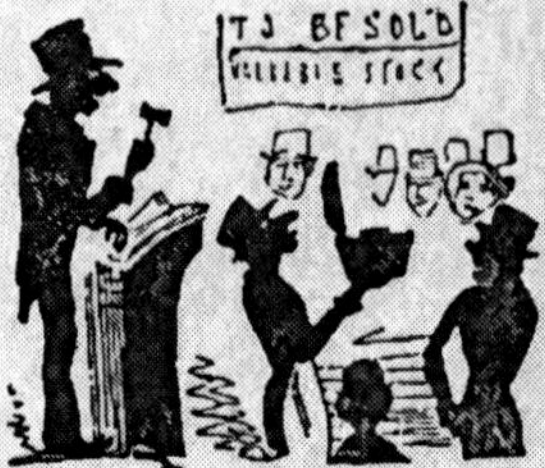

TAKING IN SAIL

I've had my dignity lowered quite enough as it is!

Alf. But look 'ere, my dear girl, I can't leave you here all by yourself you know!

Miss S. I dare say Mr. Perkins will take care of me.

[*Mr. P. assents, with effusion.*

Alf (*watching them move away—with bitterness*). I wish all Niggers were put down by Act of Parliament, I do! Downright noosances—that's what *they* are!

"DELAYS ARE DANGEROUS.—*Young Housekeeper.* "I'm afraid those soles I bought of you yesterday were not fresh. My husband said they were not nice at all!"

Brighton Fisherman. "Well, marm, that be your fault—it bean't mine. I've offered 'em yer every day this week, and you might a' 'ad 'em o' Monday if you'd a loiked!"

AT MARGATE.—*Angelina* (*very poetical, surveying the rolling ocean*). "Water, water everywhere, and not a drop to drink."

Edwin (*very practical*). No drink! Now, hang it all, Angy, if I've asked you once I've asked you three times within the last five minutes to come and do a split soda and whiskey! And *I* can do with it!

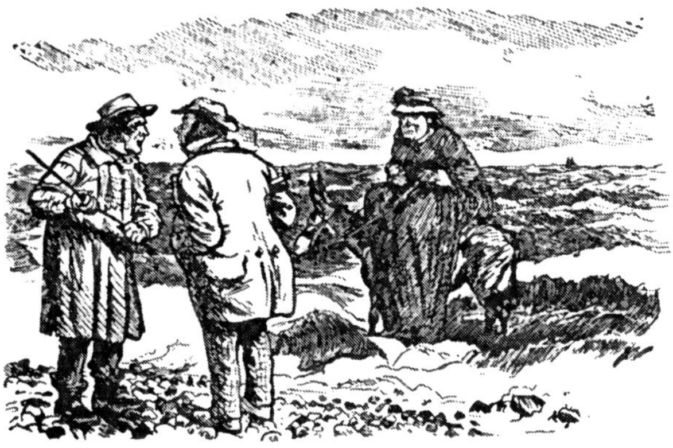

A FIX

Separated husband. "Fetch him out, sir!"
Proprietor of moke. "Why, if I went near her, she'd lie down; she always goes in just before high water; nothing'll fetch her out till the tide turns!"

THE HUSBANDS' BOAT, A MARGATE MELODY

SEE! what craft Margate Harbour displays,
  There are luggers and cutters and yawls,
They sail upon sunshiny days,
  For land-sailors arn't partial to squalls.
There's Paterfamilias takes out the lot
  Of the progeny he may own,
But the Saturday Evening boat has got
  A freight that is hers alone.
By far the most precious of craft afloat,
Is the Saturday Evening "Husbands' Boat."

There are husbands with luggage, and husbands with none,
  There are husbands with parcels in hand,
They bring down to wives whom they lately have won,
  Who pretty attentions command.
There are husbands who know whate'er time it may be
  Their wives on the jetty will wait
For that Hymeneal argosy,
  With its matrimonial freight.
Oh! the most precious of craft afloat
Is the Saturday Evening "Husbands' Boat."

But the Monday Morning is "Monday black,"
  That when at school we knew,
For the husbands to business must all go back,
  And the wives look monstrous blue;

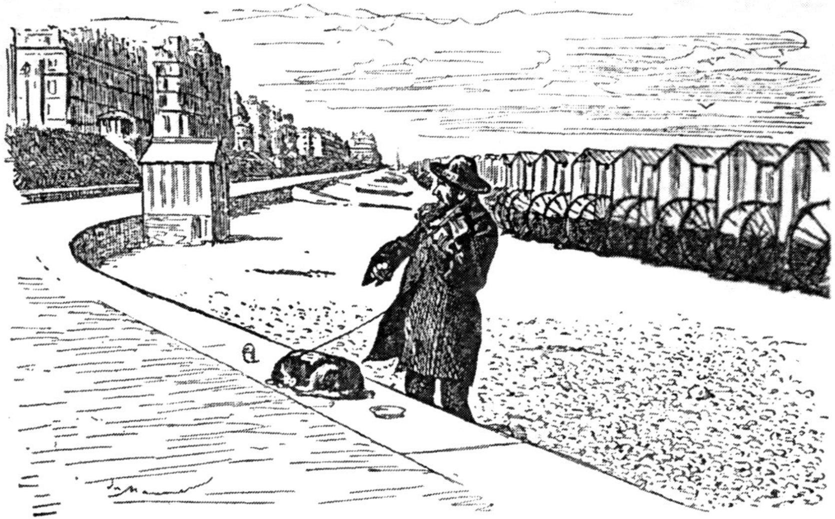

FINIS!
(THE END OF THE SEASON)

So loud the bell rings, and the steamer starts
  On her way to Thames Haven again,
And amid those who leave are as many sad hearts,
  As there are amid those who remain.
Coming or going of craft afloat,
The most prized one is the "Husbands' Boat."

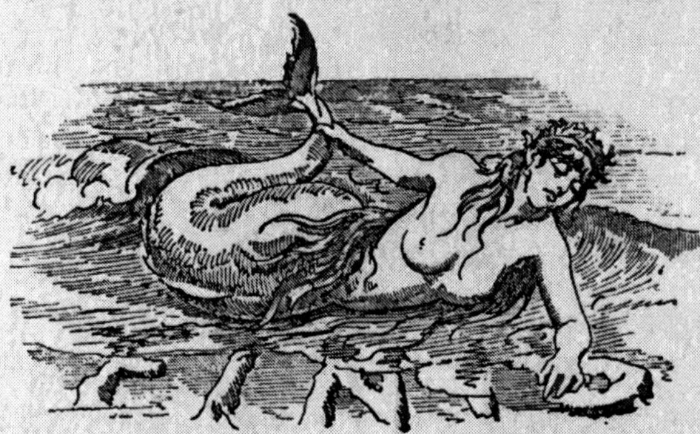

BRADBURY, AGNEW & CO. LD., PRINTERS, LONDON AND TONBRIDGE.

CPSIA information can be obtained at www.ICGtesting.com
Printed in the USA
BVOW081600280911

272358BV00014B/88/P